NEW ERA
BUSINESS ENGLISH

新时代
商务英语综合教程

学生用书 2

总主编　王立非
主　编　姚孝军
副主编　吴　彬　范　琼
原著作者　【英】Ian Wood
　　　　　【英】Anne Williams
　　　　　【英】Anna Cowper

清华大学出版社
北京

Copyright © 2017 by National Geographic Learning, a Cengage company.
Original edition published by Cengage Learning. All rights reserved.
本书原版由圣智学习出版公司出版。版权所有，盗印必究。

Tsinghua University Press is authorized by Cengage Learning to publish and distribute exclusively this adaptation edition. This edition is authorized for sale only in the People's Republic of China excluding Hong Kong SAR, Macao SAR and Taiwan Province. Unauthorized export of this edition is a violation of the Copyright Act. No part of this publication may be reproduced or distributed by any means, or stored in a database or retrieval system, without the prior written permission of the publisher.
本改编版由圣智学习出版公司授权清华大学出版社独家出版发行。此版本仅限在中华人民共和国境内（不包括中国香港、澳门特别行政区及中国台湾省）销售。未经授权的本书出口将被视为违反版权法的行为。未经出版者预先书面许可，不得以任何方式复制或发行本书的任何部分。

Cengage Learning Asia Pte. Ltd.
151 Lorong Chuan, #02-08 New Tech Park, Singapore 556741
本书封面贴有 Cengage Learning 防伪标签，无标签者不得销售。

北京市版权局著作权合同登记号　图字：01-2018-0756

版权所有，侵权必究。侵权举报电话：010-62782989 13701121933

图书在版编目（CIP）数据

新时代商务英语综合教程. 学生用书. 2 / 王立非总主编；姚孝军主编. —北京：清华大学出版社，2019
ISBN 978-7-302-52772-5

Ⅰ.①新…　Ⅱ.①王…　②姚…　Ⅲ.①商务—英语—高等学校—教材　Ⅳ.①F7

中国版本图书馆 CIP 数据核字（2019）第 077460 号

责任编辑：徐　静
封面设计：子　一
责任校对：王凤芝
责任印制：杨　艳

出版发行：清华大学出版社
　　网　　址：http://www.tup.com.cn，http://www.wqbook.com
　　地　　址：北京清华大学学研大厦A座　邮　　编：100084
　　社 总 机：010-62770175　　邮　　购：010-62786544
　　投稿与读者服务：010-62776969，c-service@tup.tsinghua.edu.cn
　　质 量 反 馈：010-62772015，zhiliang@tup.tsinghua.edu.cn
印 装 者：小森印刷（北京）有限公司
经　　销：全国新华书店
开　　本：210mm×285mm　　印　张：9.25　　字　数：246千字
版　　次：2019年6月第1版　　　　　　　印　次：2019年6月第1次印刷
定　　价：57.00元

产品编号：078729-01

Preface

改革开放 40 年，商务英语专业创办 10 年来，全国已有 367 所高校开设了商务英语本科专业，商务英语人才培养在我国已初具规模，商务英语人才培养体系不断完善，一个突出的标志就是核心课程和核心教材建设。近年来，商务英语专业教材建设的特点是：引进和原创相结合，引进了一批国际知名的经典商务英语教材，如 *Market Leader*、*Intelligent Business*、*Cambridge Business English Certificate* 等，而且，还自主开发了一批商务英语教材；其次是继承和创新相结合，在继承外语技能教学优良传统的同时，将语言、文化、商务相结合，解决了打牢英语基本功、学习文化、培养商务意识和商务素养兼顾的难题；此外，教材和课程建设同步，通过编写教材，创建了"综合商务英语"等一批新课，打造出"金课"，有力地推动了商务英语专业核心课程和教材建设。

根据 2018 年教育部颁布的《普通高等学校外国语言文学类本科专业教学质量国家标准》的要求，商务英语专业必须开设 17 门核心课程，其中最重要的一门课程就是"综合商务英语"。该课程是商务英语专业基础阶段的英语技能主干课程，对打牢学生的商务英语基本功、拓展商务文化、培养商务意识和商务素养极为重要。

针对"综合商务英语"主干核心课程，清华大学出版社引进了著名的剑桥商务英语经典教材，并按国家标准的要求，组织强大的商务英语教材编写团队，经过精心改编，推出了"新时代商务英语综合教程"。这套教材具有以下六个特点：

第一，原版引进著名的剑桥商务英语教材，该教材编写和出版质量高，在国外面世后多次再版，多年畅销，经久不衰，堪称经典。

第二，改编后的教材共分为 4 册，适合 1~2 年级"综合商务英语"课程 4 个学期使用，每学期使用 1 册。每册 8 个单元，4 册共 32 个单元，每个单元包含 2 篇课文，适用于每周 4

个学时的课堂教学使用。

第三，所有单元的主题都与真实职场和商务活动密切相关，并经过精心编排，教材主题由浅入深，既相互联系，又相对独立。课文选材短小精悍，图文并茂，语篇鲜活，可读性极强，并配有充足的练习题，练习任务设计丰富而实用，兼顾词汇、语法、听说、写作、翻译、商务知识、商务文化、商务沟通等各方面。

第四，对引进教材做适当改编，以符合中国英语教学的特点和需求。此外，还增加了全英文的商务知识点和商务翻译，前者扩展学生的商务知识，后者训练学生英汉互译的能力，弥补了教材背景知识不足、没有翻译练习的缺陷。

第五，为第3册和第4册教材精心编配了商务案例分析单元，训练学生以问题为导向，以案例为对象，提高商务环境下分析问题和解决问题的能力。

第六，针对全国商务英语专业四级考试的题型和要求，教材练习部分增加了与四级考试相关的题型，帮助学生熟悉和了解四级考试的形式和难度。

本套教材适合全国商务英语专业应用型本科院校作为"综合商务英语"课程教材使用，也适合高职高专商务英语专业选用，同时也可作为经管类专业学生的专业英语教材，以及商务英语爱好者和企业员工英语培训使用。本套教材的改编得到了对外经济贸易大学、西南财经大学、华中农业大学、山东财经大学、安徽财经大学等高校的专家和清华大学出版社的领导和编辑的大力支持，在此表示衷心感谢。

谨以此纪念改革开放40年商务英语的发展，是为序。

北京语言大学教授、博士生导师

王立非

2019年1月于北京

Contents

UNIT 1 Facts and figures — 2
- Warming up — 4
- Text A Performance — 5
- Business know-how — 11
- Text B An annual report — 12

UNIT 2 Product — 18
- Warming up — 20
- Text A The Lotus Century X Smartphone — 21
- Business know-how — 26
- Text B Drug development in the U.S.A. — 27

UNIT 3 Quality control — 34
- Warming up — 36
- Text A Monitoring quality — 36
- Business know-how — 42
- Text B Improving quality — 43

UNIT 4 The call centre — 50

    Warming up — 52
    Text A The call centre — 52
    Business know-how — 59
    Text B Call centre creates 2,000 jobs in the Philippines — 60

Review Test 1 — 66

UNIT 5 Banking — 74

    Warming up — 76
    Text A Internet banking — 76
    Business know-how — 81
    Text B The banking revolution — 82

UNIT 6 Trading — 88

    Warming up — 90
    Text A An import agent — 90
    Business know-how — 98
    Text B Quotation — 99

UNIT 7 Delivery services — 104

- Warming up — 106
- **Text A** Parcel carriers — 106
- Business know-how — 111
- **Text B** Sending a parcel — 112

UNIT 8 Recruiting staff — 118

- Warming up — 120
- **Text A** Advertising a vacancy — 121
- Business know-how — 126
- **Text B** Recruitment methods — 127

Review Test 2 — 134

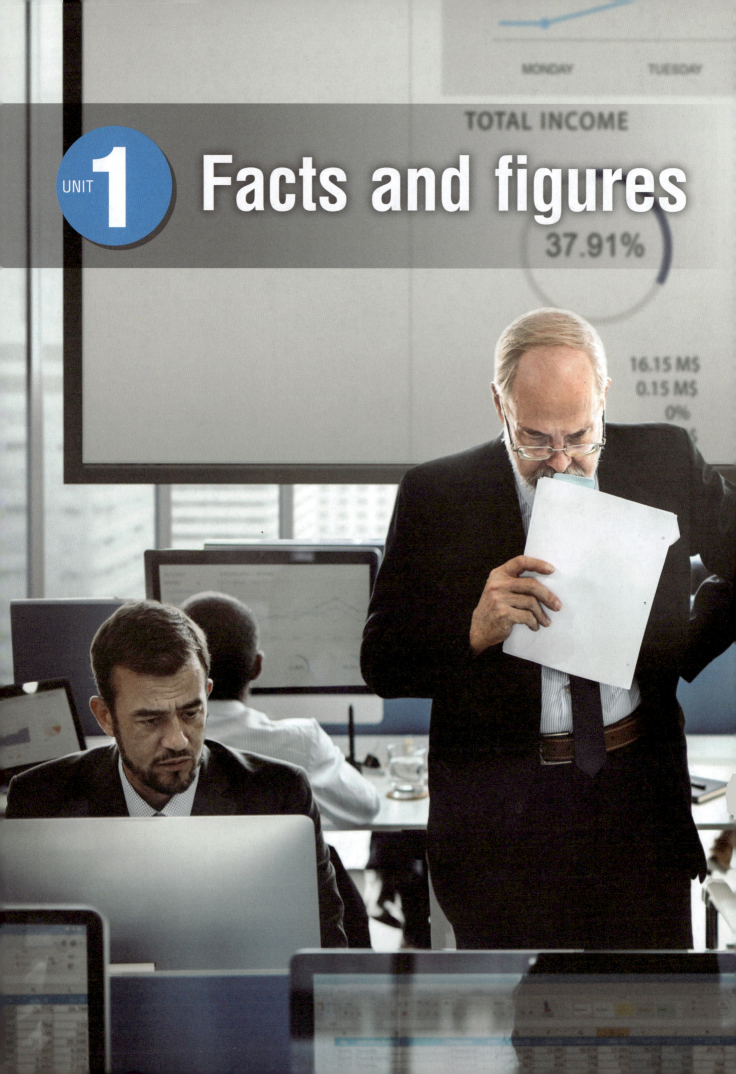

Warming up

TASK 1 Look at the charts below. They show the orders for eight different companies over three years. Which company does each sentence describe? For each sentence mark the correct letter. Do not use any letter more than once.

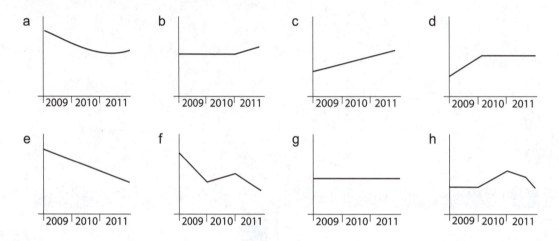

1. After a sharp drop in 2009, orders recovered for twelve months and then fell again in 2011.
2. Orders rose sharply in 2010 but peaked at the end of the year and then fell back to their 2009 levels.
3. Orders remained steady between 2009 and 2011.
4. The order books showed strong growth throughout the three-year period.
5. After decreasing steadily for two years, orders finally levelled off and began a recovery in 2011.

TASK 2 Match the names with the diagrams. Which diagrams could be used to show 1–8?

bar chart   pie chart   flow chart   graph

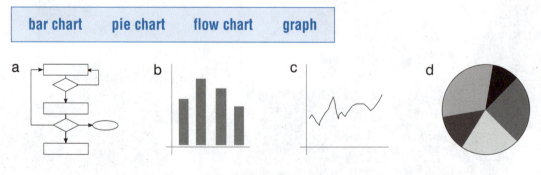

1. sales growth
2. a breakdown of costs
3. a production process
4. profits over several years
5. market share
6. the number of employees
7. share price performance
8. income per product as a % of turnover

Text A Performance

Railwork West is one of twenty-eight private rail companies operating in Britain. The company's Communications Manager, Shelley Cohen, makes a presentation to possible investors.

Good afternoon. My name is Shelley Cohen and I'm here to talk about Railwork West's performance. As you all know, Railwork West has only been a private company since the privatisation of the national railway network in 1997.

Between 1997 and 2007, Railwork West was owned and run by the Conaxus Group. However, the period of change from publicly-owned transport system to private company was not an easy one. Conaxus had considerable problems—asset management was difficult, passenger revenues fell and customer satisfaction dropped dramatically. In 2007, Transcon bought Railwork West and since that time, we have made a lot of changes. Today I'd like to talk to you about these changes and show you how they've affected the company's performance since 2006. To do this, I'd like to draw your attention to figures three and four on Page 8 of your information brochures.

I'd like to begin with a look at the bar chart, which shows annual growth in passenger revenue from 2006 to 2010. As you can see, growth slowed from 2.4% in 2006/2007 down to just 1% in 2007/2008. However, reduced costs and more efficient sales practices resulted in growth reaching 9.9% in 2008/2009. This was followed by 7% in 2009/2010. The bar chart clearly shows that the changes have made a big difference financially and have improved customer satisfaction, as we'll see.

I'm sure you've all heard the recent stories in the media about bad service on the privatised rail network, so I'd like you to look at Figure 4, which shows Railwork West's reliability and punctuality figures. As you can see from this graph, the company has an excellent reliability record. Reliability improved steadily from 99.1% in 2006 to 99.3% in 2008, where it has remained. Punctuality also rose steadily, going from 90% in 2006 to 91% in 2008. You'll notice the drop to 88% in 2009, which I'll explain later. Although we haven't received the final figures yet, I can tell you that punctuality improved in 2010 and has continued to improve this year as a result of further investment.

"Transcons is transforming the Railwork West network and bringing it into the 21st century."

Shelley Cohen
Communications Manager

Transcon bought Railwork West in 2007 after a difficult period for the company, following its privatisation ten years earlier. However, after a period of investment and rationalization, the figures below show changes in the performance of Railwork West over the last four years.

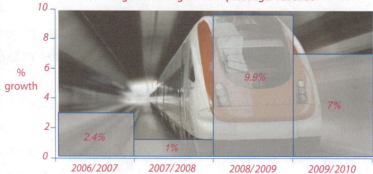

Fig.3 Annual growth in passenger revenue

- 2006/2007: 2.4%
- 2007/2008: 1%
- 2008/2009: 9.9%
- 2009/2010: 7%

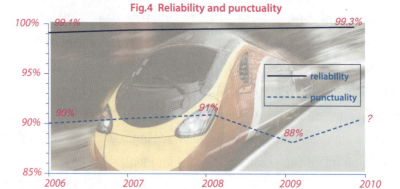

Fig.4 Reliability and punctuality

- reliability: 99.1% (2006) → 99.3% (2010)
- punctuality: 90% (2006), 91% (2008), 88% (2009), ? (2010)

Railwork West   page 8

Words and expressions

brochure /'brəʊʃə(r)/	n.	小册子，介绍手册	
considerable /kən'sɪdərəbl/	adj.	相当多的；相当大的	
dramatically /drə'mætɪkəlɪ/	adv.	显著地	
figure /'fɪɡə(r)/	n.	图形；数字	
graph /ɡrɑːf/	n.	图表；曲线图	
privatisation /ˌpraɪvətaɪ'zeɪʃən/	n.	私有化	
punctuality /ˌpʌŋktʃʊ'ælətɪ/	n.	准时	
reliability /rɪˌlaɪə'bɪlətɪ/	n.	可靠性；可靠度	
annual growth		年增长	
asset management		资产管理	
bar chart		条形图	
customer satisfaction		客户满意度	
result in		结果是，导致	

Comprehension tasks

TASK 1 Read the text and retell the information conveyed by the figures.

TASK 2 Read the text again and answer the following questions.

1. When did Railwork West become a private company?
2. What is the name of its parent company?
3. How did the company increase revenues in 2008/2009?
4. Why have some rail companies been in the newspapers recently?
5. Why has Shelley not given the punctuality figure for 2010?

Vocabulary

TASK 3 Write the words and phrases in the correct groups.

~~succeed~~	fail	beat	behind	ahead
break even	overtake	on target	disappointing	

positive	neutral	negative
succeed		

TASK 4 Complete the following Chairman's Statement with the words in the box.

> strategy   acquisition   announcement   savings
> expansion   opportunity   recovery   achievement

Chairman's Statement 2010

Last year the board promised a ¹ ___strategy___ that would focus on maximising profits. Our efforts resulted in a $15m reduction in costs. These ² _____ give us the ³ _____ to invest in the new machinery necessary to further increase our efficiency. We are sure you will agree that this was quite a(an) ⁴ _____. This new strategy meant we decided not to proceed with the planned $20m ⁵ _____ of Greystones, a west coast engineering company. Instead, we decided to focus on ⁶ _____ through increasing sales in our most important markets. This change of focus also produced a(an) ⁷ _____ of the Cumberland share price on the New York Stock Exchange, which was 40% down on the previous year. The ⁸ _____ of the withdrawal from the Greystones takeover in the financial press in early March resulted in an immediate 25% rise in the price of Cumberland shares.

TASK 5 Which word is the odd one out?

1. goal	objective	(sales)	target
2. graph	prediction	chart	diagram
3. profit	expenditure	overheads	costs
4. value	turnover	income	earnings
5. result	forecast	prediction	budget
6. current	present	existing	previous
7. capital	project	finance	assets
8. possibility	chance	position	opportunity

Listening

TASK 6 Shelley Cohen finishes her presentation and the investors ask her questions. Listen and complete the notes below.

Punctuality in 2009?

Investment plans?

Profits in the future?

TASK 7 Listen again and choose the correct option to complete each sentence.

1. The railway track that Railwork West uses belongs to
   a. the company.   b. another private company.   c. the Government.
2. The company is spending £9m in order to
   a. improve the condition of the track.
   b. build new stations and improve punctuality.
   c. improve customer service and reliability.
3. The company's biggest costs are paying
   a. other companies for the track and trains.
   b. the Government so it can operate services.
   c. for new stations and facilities.

Business communication

TASK 8 Work in pairs. Write five results or consequences that have happened in a company you know on a piece of paper. Give the paper to your partner. Find out the reasons for the results and changes.

Translation

TASK 9 Translate the following sentences into Chinese.

1. However, the period of change from publicly-owned transport system to private company was not an easy one.

2. The bar chart clearly shows that the changes have made a big difference financially and have improved customer satisfaction.

3. I'm sure you've all heard the recent stories in the media about bad service on the privatised rail network, so I'd like you to look at Figure 4, which shows Railwork West's reliability and punctuality figures.

4. The China-Europe freight trains, which focus mainly on exporting equipment and manufacturing products, reported a cargo volume of 51,400 tons—a 3.3-fold increase than before.

5. Alibaba has been crowned the most valuable brand in China for the first time in the annual ranking, having grown its brand value by 59 percent year-on-year to $141 billion.

TASK 10 Translate the following sentences into English.

1. 公司可以利用资产管理工具确切地找出在已安装的设备中有哪些硬件和软件。（asset management）

2. 客户投诉是客户满意度低的常见指标，但没有投诉并不一定意味着客户满意度高。（customer satisfaction）

3. 尽管公司已经尝试了很多补救措施，销售业绩依然显著下滑。(drop dramatically)

4. 我们所有市场去年的销售数字都显示在这个条形图上。(bar chart)

5. 他们的地方财政收入持续增长，年增长率为 12.9%。(annual growth)

Writing

TASK 11 Write a short report of the performance of a company you know.

Business know-how

Read the following passage and make an oral summary of the main points to your partner or group.

Balance sheet (资产负债表)

In financial accounting, a balance sheet or statement of financial position is a summary of the financial balances of an individual or organisation, whether it is a sole proprietorship, a business partnership, a corporation, a private limited company or other organisations such as Government or not-for-profit entity. Assets (资产), liabilities (负债) and ownership equity (所有者权益) are listed as of a specific date, such as the end of its financial year. A balance sheet is often described as a "snapshot of a company's financial condition". Of the four basic financial statements, the balance sheet is the only statement which applies to a single point in time of a business' calendar year.

A standard company balance sheet has two sides: assets, on the left and financing, which itself has two parts, liabilities and ownership equity, on the right. The main categories of assets are usually listed first, and typically in order of liquidity. Assets are followed by the liabilities. The difference between the assets and the liabilities is known as equity or the net assets or the net worth or capital of the company. According to the accounting equation, net worth must equal assets minus liabilities.

Another way to look at the balance sheet equation is that total assets equals liabilities plus owner's equity. Looking at the equation in this way shows how assets were financed: either by borrowing money (liability) or by using the owner's money (owner's or shareholders' equity). Balance sheets are usually presented with assets in one section and liabilities and net worth in the other section with the two sections "balancing".

A business operating entirely in cash can measure its profits by withdrawing (提取；撤回) the entire bank balance at the end of the period, plus any cash in hand. However, many businesses are not paid immediately; they build up inventories of goods and they acquire buildings and equipment. In other words: businesses have assets and so they cannot, even if they want to, immediately turn these into cash at the end of each period. Often, these businesses owe money to suppliers and to tax authorities, and the proprietors (所有者；经营者) do not withdraw all their original capital and profits at the end of each period. In other words, businesses also have liabilities.

Text B An annual report

Here is the extract from the Annual Report of U.K.-based video-games developer Kobra Arts.

Chairman's Statement

Last year saw both the continued development of trends within the industry and some unexpected results. Domestic sales in the U.K. continued to grow, but could be overtaken by U.S.A. sales next year. As in 2009, sales in the U.S.A. rose sharply with the successful release of American versions of best-selling games like *Virtual Ninja* and *Law and Order* for PlayStation 3 and Xbox 360. However, the European market fell slightly at the beginning of the year due to the global economic crisis, but then remained steady.

Sports titles increased their domination of sales of new games in 2010 with the football game *Football Maniacs* selling over 800,000 units in World Cup year. We plan to further develop our range of sports simulation games over the next five years.

The company has also enjoyed a sharp rise in sales of educational products. Our new range of interactive multimedia products, *SupaSchool*, launched in late 2009, is now a top-selling brand. Further *SupaSchool* titles to be launched this year should ensure continued growth in this market.

Sales figures for 2010 show very clearly the changing face of the company's activities. 70% of Kobra's revenue now comes from action and simulation games developed primarily for portable games consoles. In order to maintain our profile in this highly competitive market, the company will have to expand by increasing its range of new games and reducing its development times.

Moreover, the company faces new challenges in distribution. Online superstores now account for almost 40% of the sales of our computer games. They offer a narrow product range, based on top-selling titles, at extremely competitive prices which eat into profit margins. There is also a strong second-hand market. Gamers are buying and selling their old games online and this may be affecting sales of our most established games.

David Matthews

David Matthews, Chairman

Annual Report 2010

2010 distribution
- Others 5%
- Department stores 5%
- Independent 7%
- Wholesalers 19%
- Online stores 39%
- Computer shops 25%

Top selling Kobra Arts titles 2010

Title	Units
Football Maniacs	850,000
Sports Pro 500	796,000
Golf Go!	460,000
Law & Order II	348,000
Virtual Ninja	239,000
Hero City	122,000

Sales per platform as %
- PlayStation 3 — 42%
- Xbox 360 — 28%
- PCs — 24%
- Sega Genesis — 6%

Words and expressions

best-selling /best 'selɪŋ/	adj. 畅销的	revenue /'revənjuː/	n. 收入；收益
distribution /ˌdɪstrɪ'bjuːʃən/	n. 经销；分销	simulation /ˌsɪmjʊ'leɪʃən/	n. 模拟；仿真
domination /ˌdɒmɪ'neɪʃən/	n. 支配, 主宰	top-selling /tɒp'selɪŋ/	adj. 畅销的
established /ɪ'stæblɪʃt/	adj. 稳固的；成熟的	trend /trend/	n. 趋势
extremely /ɪk'striːmlɪ/	adv. 极其, 非常	account for	（数量、比例方面）占
interactive /ˌɪntər'æktɪv/	adj. 交互的	domestic sales	国内销售
overtake /ˌəʊvə'teɪk/	v. 超过	due to	由于，因为
portable /'pɔːtəbl/	adj. 便于携带的	eat into	侵蚀；消耗
primarily /'praɪmərəlɪ/	adv. 首要地, 主要地	games console	游戏机；游戏控制台
profile /'prəʊfaɪl/	n. 形象	profit margin	边际利润
release /rɪ'liːs/	n. 发布；发行	sales figures	销售数据

Comprehension tasks

 Read the text and answer the following questions.

1. What type of software does the company manufacture?
2. Was 2010 a good year?
3. Would you invest in the company? Why/Why not?

 Say whether the following sentences are "Right" or "Wrong" according to the text. If there is not enough information to answer, write "Doesn't say".

1. Online superstores sell more Kobra products than computer shops. _____
2. PCs are the most widely-used platform for Kobra games. _____
3. Sales increased sharply in the company's home market last year. _____
4. *Football Maniacs* sold more copies in South Africa than in Britain. _____
5. The company is developing its range of multimedia educational software. _____
6. In future the company will have to produce new games more quickly. _____
7. Online superstores sell a wide range of computer games. _____

Vocabulary

 Use the following words and phrases to label the diagrams.

| peak | remain steady | fall | rise | level off | recover |

a ⬊ b ⬈ c ➝ d ➝ e ⬊ f ⬇

Complete the following sentences with the prepositions in the box.

| in | at | by | from | of |

1. Last year there was a drop _____ net sales _____ 9%.
2. Market share increased _____ 3%, up to 8%.
3. Net sales peaked _____ £22m in 2007.

4. European sales went _____ £4.2m to £3.0m.
5. Sales levelled off _____ £5m in 2008.
6. Costs rose _____ £3.3m. This was a rise _____ 10%.
7. Office software sales fell _____ 10% in 2007.
8. A strong pound meant a fall _____ exports in 2008.

TASK 5 Match the following words by use of linking lines.

1. retail — brand
2. product — chain
3. net — income
4. top-selling — report
5. annual — launch

Speaking

TASK 6 Work in groups. Students in each group take turns to retell **Text B** and the rest ask some relevant questions about the report as the audience.

TASK 7 Form a pair and discuss the following topic with your partner.

What type of information should be contained in a company's annual report?

Business communication

TASK 8 Find people in your group who have done the things below. Then ask three follow-up questions. Find someone who has…

- been to a conference this year.
- changed jobs this year.
- worked in a foreign country.
- done some kind of training this year.
- been promoted in the last five years.

Speaking tip:
To keep a conversation going, follow up all yes/no questions with more open questions (when? why? how? etc.).

Translation

 Translate the following sentences into Chinese.

1. In order to maintain our profile in this highly competitive market, the company will have to expand by increasing its range of new games and reducing its development times.

2. They offer a narrow product range, based on top-selling titles, at extremely competitive prices which eat into profit margins.

3. However, the European market fell slightly at the beginning of the year due to the global economic crisis, but then remained steady.

4. According to the China Association of Automobile Manufacturers, total vehicle sales in first quarter stood at 6.37 million units, a decline of 11.32 percent compared with last year.

5. By contrast, BYD, China's leading new energy vehicle manufacturer, reported a year-on-year 632 percent increase in net profit for the first quarter of 2019 on the back of boom in the new energy vehicle sales.

 Translate the following sentences into English.

1. 尽管该公司的商用飞机业务在近期利润大幅上升，但其收入却一直在下降。(rise sharply)

2. 这家公司调查了市场需求，决定推出新产品。(launch)

3. 协议为双方就产品分销与技术开发订立了合作安排。(distribution)

4. SANA 是新加坡最大和最成熟的几个社会福利机构之一。(most established)

5. 非常高兴地告诉您，你们的"永久"牌自行车已成为我方市场上最畅销的品牌之一。(best-selling)

Writing

TASK 11 Write a short description of the graph below.

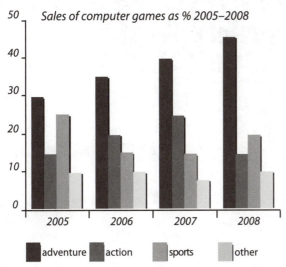

Sales of computer games as % 2005–2008

adventure ■ action ■ sports ■ other

Unit 1 Facts and figures

UNIT 2 Product

Warming up

TASK 1 Robert Saunders, the Sales Manager at Columbine Games, talks about two new products. Listen to his presentation. Which products does he talk about? How much do they cost?

TASK 2 Listen to the presentation again. The speaker refers to the following things. What is he talking about?

1. General knowledge
2. Size, weight and cost
3. Wood
4. 23 cm x 23 cm
5. 300 grammes
6. €14.99

Text A: The Lotus Century X Smartphone

The new Lotus Century X is the latest addition to our extensive range of mobile technology devices. It is probably the most advanced smartphone on the market today. The wide range of cutting-edge features includes a four-inch AMOLED display screen, HD video recording, camera phone and many apps. Improved technology means that the screen is now 20% brighter, the colours are 20% clearer and the screen is 80% more responsive to the touch. Furthermore, the 1GHZ processor uses less power than many other models; as a result the Lotus Century X is one of the cheapest smartphones to use. The five megapixel camera is also an HD video recorder and Lotus DNA convergence technology allows you to take videos and send them to a compatible TV. Finally, the Lotus Century X hub technology puts all your social media contacts, such as Facebook, Twitter or LinkedIn into one place, so it really does make your life easier, both at work and at home.

Words and expressions

app (=application) /æp/	n.	手机应用软件	
compatible /kəm'pætəbl/	adj.	兼容的；相容的	
cutting-edge /'kʌtɪŋ'edʒ/	adj.	高端的；最前沿的	
display /dɪ'spleɪ/	n.	显示器	
extensive /ɪk'stensɪv/	adj.	广泛的	
furthermore /ˌfɜːðə'mɔː(r)/	adv.	此外；与此同时	
hub /hʌb/	n.	集线器	
megapixel /'megəpɪksl/	n.	百万像素，兆像素	
processor /'prəʊsesə(r)/	n.	处理器	
responsive /rɪ'spɒnsɪv/	adj.	反应灵敏的	
screen /skriːn/	n.	屏幕	
smartphone /'smɑːtfəʊn/	n.	智能手机	
convergence technology		融合技术	
HD (=high definition)		高清晰度	
social media		社交媒体	

Comprehension tasks

Task 1 Read the text and answer the following questions.

1. What are the cutting-edge features of the new Lotus Century X smartphone?

Unit 2 Product 21

2. What does improved technology for the Lotus Century X mean?
3. Why is the Lotus Century X one of the cheapest smartphones to use?
4. What allows you to take videos and send them to a compatible TV?

 Read the text again and circle "True" or "False". Correct the false sentences.

1. The new Lotus Century X is probably the most advanced smartphone on the market today and in the future. True/False
2. The 1GHZ processor of the Lotus Century X uses more power than many other models. True/False
3. The screen of the new Lotus Century X is now 20% brighter, the colours are 20% clearer and the screen is 80% more responsive to the touch. True/False
4. The Lotus Century X is one of the most expensive smartphones to use. True/False
5. The Lotus Century X hub technology puts all your social media contacts into one place. True/False

Vocabulary

 Complete the following sentences with the correct form of the words in the box.

| cheap | contact | advance | latest | improved | mobile | extensive |

1. _____ reports say that another ten people have been killed.
2. In a(an) _____ society, people move easily from one job, home, or social class to another.
3. Without more training or _____ technical skills, they'll lose their jobs.
4. If they need help or have questions, is all of your _____ information up to date and easy to find?
5. I'm going to live off campus if I can find somewhere _____ enough.
6. This was an important event because the U.S. was seeking to _____ relations with a Communist country during the Cold War.
7. It can be used for a(an) _____ range of products including drinks, cream, milk, sauces, soups and liquid desserts.

Match the opposite adjectives by use of linking lines. Then use one of each pair to complete the sentences.

positive	negative
huge	heavy
brand new	tiny
exciting	weak
reliable	ugly
attractive	out of date
strong	expensive
economical	boring
portable	defective

1. Compared to the huge old version, this one's ___tiny___.
2. The S2000 is _____ so you can carry it with you wherever you go.
3. Its design had become _____ so we had to stop making it.
4. Low fuel consumption makes it one of the most _____ cars on the road.
5. We had to withdraw the new product due to a(an) _____ component.
6. Customers found the design sample _____ and lacking any real interest.
7. Most people thought it looked ugly but some found it very _____.
8. Its ultra-hard (硬度高的) plastic casing (外壳) means it's very _____.

Complete the warranty with the words and phrases in the box.

guarantee	replacement	consumer	customer service
return	condition	wear and tear	non-standard

   Under the terms of this (1) _____, the customer has the right to (2) _____ any product that is defective or in a poor (3) _____. This does not apply to any product that has suffered natural (4) _____ or has been damaged through negligence or fitted with (5) _____ parts as the result of a customer installation.

   All damaged or faulty goods should be sent to the (6) _____ department and you will be issued with a (7) _____ product of the same type. This will not affect your (8) _____ rights.

Listening

TASK 6 A medical journalist asks a marketing manager about a new drug for arthritis. Listen and answer the questions.

1. What is the drug called?
2. Who is the drug for?
3. Where will patients be able to get the drug?
4. What are the possible side effects?
5. How will patients get information about the drug?

TASK 7 Listen again and note down any dates you hear. Then put the actions below into the correct order.

- ☐ give general information posters to doctors
- ☐ visit doctors to talk about the product
- ☐ launch the drug
- ☐ give information leaflets to patients
- ☐ send information packs to doctors   *(end of April)*

Business communication

TASK 8 Work in pairs. Think of something you have both bought. Make a list of the points you considered when you bought it. Discuss the importance of the points and put them in order. Then prepare to report back to the rest of the group.

Product name: _____

Points considered	Me	My partner
price		

Translation

 Translate the following sentences into Chinese.

1. The wide range of cutting-edge features includes a four-inch AMOLED display screen, HD video recording, camera phone and many apps.

2. Furthermore, the 1GHZ processor uses less power than many other models; as a result the Lotus Century X is one of the cheapest smartphones to use.

3. Finally, the Lotus Century X hub technology puts all your social media contacts, such as Facebook, Twitter or LinkedIn into one place, so it really does make your life easier, both at work and at home.

4. The company lags far behind its competitors, such as Apple and Samsung, and currently accounts for just 5% of the smartphone market in the world.

5. Microsoft spent an estimated $7bn to develop Vista, but software security problems have delayed the product launch for more than two years.

 Translate the following sentences into English.

1. 我们正在研发的是一种在美国从未使用过的尖端技术。(cutting-edge)

2. 随着互联网的普及和通信方式的改进，全球市场的反应也变得更为灵敏。(responsive)

3. 老师在点名时，竟然把我的名字误认为是男孩的名字，结果他们都笑了。(as a result)

4. 这个电脑设备与那个软件不兼容，因此不能一起使用。(compatible)

5. 布朗先生赢得了各地农场主的尊重，而且，他们很信任他。(furthermore)

Unit 2 Product 25

Writing

 Write about a product that you have recently bought.

- Where was it made?
- What is it made of?
- Why did you buy it instead of a similar product?

Business know-how

Read the following passage and make an oral summary of the main points to your partner or group.

Product launch（产品发布）

Product launch is the process of introducing a new product for sale for the first time and attracting people's attention to it. It can be an existing product which is already in the market or it can be a completed new innovative product which the company has made. Product launch involves various steps, such as understanding customer needs, product design, testing of the product, marketing & advertising and ensuring that the product reaches out to all its audience. A successful product launch provides a sales momentum（动力）for the company.

The principles of a successful product launch are the following:

a. relating product capabilities to market needs;
b. having a clear positioning and messaging（消息传递）tagline（宣传词）;
c. setting clear goals for launch;
d. having the power of leverage（影响力）;
e. having a proper time of launch.

The steps to have a successful launch are as below:

a. designing attractive packaging;
b. determining the target segment（目标客群）;
c. having a unique slogan;
d. knowing the potential competitors;
e. consulting a public relations firm;

f. creating a product sheet having the list of product features. This sheet would explain the product to the customers and make it capable for purchase;

g. launching a website of the company (if it is not existent);

h. placing ads in several media outlets in order to maximise the reach. Online ads can also be useful;

i. finally holding a press conference that addresses the media about the product features.

Text B — Drug development in the U.S.A.

The development of new drugs is essential if we are to stop the spread of diseases. However, it takes an average of twelve to fifteen years to develop a drug and it costs a company from $500m to over $1bn. Only five out of every 5,000 drugs that start the testing process are tested on humans. Only one in five of those actually reaches the market.

There are four stages of testing a new drug. First of all, a company carries out tests for about two and a half years in the laboratory and on animals. This is to show how the drug works against a particular disease and to show its level of safety. Then testing on humans can begin.

The first stage of human testing tests the safety of the drug on fewer than one hundred healthy people and lasts about a year. After that, the drug is tested for about two years on 100–300 people who suffer from the disease to see how well the drug works. The final stage lasts about three years: the drug is usually tested on 1,000–3,000 patients in hospitals and clinics. While they are carrying out these tests, doctors monitor the patient closely and keep a record of the success of the drug and any side-effects.

When a company has completed the three stages of tests on humans, the company makes a New Drug Application to the FDA (Food and Drug Administration), which is often 1,000 pages or more.

How long the FDA takes to review a New Drug Application depends on many things. Sometimes, important new discoveries are "fast-tracked"; the average review time is 29.9 months.

When the FDA has approved the New Drug Application, doctors can finally give it to their patients. The company still keeps a quality control record of the drug, including any side-effects.

Discovering and developing safe and successful new drugs is a long, difficult and expensive process. America's pharmaceutical companies spent $65bn last year on developing new drugs. Companies invest up to 18% of their sales on research and the high investment is likely to continue.

Words and expressions

average	/ˈævərɪdʒ/	n. 平均数	be likely to		很可能
		adj. 平均的	carry out		实行；开展
clinic	/ˈklɪnɪk/	n. 诊所	FDA (Food and Drug Administration)		（美国）食品及药物管理局
closely	/ˈkləʊsli/	adv. 密切地			
fast-track	/ˈfɑːstˈtræk/	adj. 优先处理的；快速处理的	keep a record of		把……记录下来
side-effect	/ˈsaɪdɪˈfekt/	n. （药物的）副作用	New Drug Application		新药上市申请

Comprehension tasks

 Read the text and complete the table below.

	Laboratory	People		
		Stage 1	Stage 2	Stage 3
Test period:				
Tested on:				
Reason for testing:				

 Read the text again and answer the following questions.

1. How many years of testing are there before a drug reaches the market?
2. What do doctors do while they are carrying out tests on patients in hospitals?
3. What is the first stage of testing a new drug according to the text?
4. When can a company make a New Drug Application to the FDA?
5. What percentage of turnover (营业额) do companies invest in research of new drugs?

Vocabulary

TASK 3 Complete the following sentences with the suitable words.

1. We'll have to _____ sales of this new product for several months.
   a. monitor   b. look   c. see
2. I'm afraid that product isn't _____ until next week.
   a. free   b. available   c. public
3. Today, the number of our domestic group purchase websites has been _____ more than 1,000 and is in constant growth.
   a. up to   b. down to   c. on to
4. They plan to ask the Food and Drug Administration to _____ the new drug in the next few months.
   a. take   b. approve   c. produce
5. Our company is _____ a new product in spring.
   a. launching   b. bringing   c. giving

TASK 4 Complete the following sentences with the correct form of the words and phrases in the box.

| average | be likely to | closely | carry out |
| developed | fast-track | make an application | |

1. If you can spend more time, you _____ pass the English final examination.
2. His innovation caught the attention of the relevant departments and it was _____.
3. You'll need to _____ to your teacher in advance for your personal leave.
4. We have pleasure in sending our catalog（商品目录）and price list of newly _____ products.
5. In the past ten years, the economy of this country has expanded by a(an) _____ of 3.7% a year, twice the rate of the whole Eurozone.
6. China will further _____ open-door policy to promote the economic contacts with other countries in the world.
7. Today, the United States and India are working together more _____ than ever to keep their people safe.

Match the verbs or phrasal verbs with the nouns by use of linking lines.

1. develop — papers
2. make — a drug
3. review — a disease
4. carry out — a patient
5. suffer from — an application
6. monitor — a record
7. keep — a test

Speaking

Work in pairs. Discuss what you would like to know when you buy a mobile phone.

- What is the size of the product?
- How many colours does it come in?
- How heavy is it?
- What are the main features of it?
- How much does it cost?
- How long is the warranty（保修期）?

Form a pair and discuss the following topic with your partner.

Make a brief introduction of a board game that you like.

Business communication

Task 8 Work in pairs. Look at the following cards and ask your partner questions about his/her plans for the future.

work schedule for the next week

personal plans for the weekend

plans for the next six months

work schedule for the next six months

business trip

holiday

Translation

Task 9 Translate the following sentences into Chinese.

1. Only five out of every 5,000 drugs that start the testing process are tested on humans. Only one in five of those actually reaches the market.

2. While they are carrying out these tests, doctors monitor the patient closely and keep a record of the success of the drug and any side-effects.

3. When a company has completed the three stages of tests on humans, the company makes a New Drug Application to the FDA (Food and Drug Administration), which is often 1,000 pages or more.

4. The supplier was contacted as we wanted to make a change to our order and fortunately they were kind and willing to help.

5. Drug development is a high cost and labourious (耗时费力的) process, requiring a number of tests until a drug is made available in the market.

 Translate the following sentences into English.

1. 中国的人均水资源供给仅为全球平均水平的1/4。(average)

2. 他说公司已经向投资审查委员会表达了尽快做出决定的重要性。(review)

3. 如果父母有读书的习惯，他们的孩子将很有可能向他们学习。(be likely to)

4. 我会把他所有的通话都记录下来。(keep a record of)

5. 一般来说，如果按照说明服用，这种药没有副作用。(side-effect)

Writing

 Work in pairs or groups. Look at the cards describing drug development. Put the stages in order. Then write a description of the process.

- The company keeps a record of test results for the authorities.
- The company finishes tests on humans.
- The company tests the new drugs on animals.
- The company tests the drug on a larger number of patients.
- The authorities approve the drug.
- The company can launch the drug.

| The company tests the new drug on healthy people to check safety. | The company applies to the authorities for approval. | The company tests the new drug on a small number of patients to see how well it works. |

Unit 2 Product 33

UNIT 3 Quality control

Warming up

 1 What is Quality Control (QC)? Discuss with your partner and take notes.

 2 Discuss with your partner what the job of a QC manager at a snacks factory involves. Use the words in the box.

| check | monitor | inspect | sample | reject |

Text A Monitoring quality

Mazli Amhar is Head of Quality Control at Alibaba, a Malaysian snack producer. She talks about monitoring quality.

Visitor Could you tell me a bit about quality control at the factory?

Mazli Well, there are four main quality control inspection points. We begin by visiting our suppliers to make sure we are happy with their quality control. Next, we inspect all goods in on arrival at our factory and the third inspection point is during production. And the final stage is chemical analysis of our finished goods.

Visitor And what do you look for at each of the four inspection points?

Mazli Well, each stage is different. With our suppliers, for instance, we inspect their QC processes and, even more importantly, their factory hygiene. If we're not happy with their hygiene, we'll cancel the supply contract. At the goods in stage we make sure that order quantities are correct and the quality is OK. We also check the transport packaging. If the packaging is damaged, the warehouse shelf-life can be reduced.

Visitor And what quality checks do you run during production?

Mazli We take samples to check there isn't too much cooking oil on the snack and that each snack has the minimum amount of flavouring. We also check the size of the snacks and their crispness. If the snacks are too oily, they go soft.

Visitor	So that leaves the finished goods. What do you check for at the final QC stage?
Mazli	We check individual bags to make sure that the packet weight is above the acceptable minimum and that the packet is sealed properly. We also check the taste.
Visitor	And how do you do that?
Mazli	Well, we eat them. How else? We also do chemical analysis to check things like fat levels and other information that we have to put on the packets.

Words and expressions

flavouring /ˈfleɪvərɪŋ/ n. 调味品
hygiene /ˈhaɪdʒiːn/ n. 卫生
inspect /ɪnˈspekt/ v. 检查；检验
packaging /ˈpækɪdʒɪŋ/ n. 外包装
sample /ˈsæmpl/ n. 样品
seal /siːl/ v. 密封
shelf-life /ˈʃelflaɪf/ n. 保质期，货架期
warehouse /ˈweəhaʊs/ n. 仓库

chemical analysis 化学分析
fat level 脂肪含量
finished goods 制成品
inspection point 检查点；检验点
order quantity 订购量
packet weight 包装重量
supply contract 供应合同

Comprehension tasks

Read the text and complete the table below.

Quality Control at Alibaba

Inspection points

1 Suppliers	2 Goods in	3 _____	4 Finished goods
• QC processes	• quantities	• cooking oil	• _____
• _____	• _____	• flavouring	• packet seal
	• _____	• _____	• _____
		• crispness	

Unit 3 Quality control 37

Read the text again and answer the following questions.

1. Why is hygiene very important for the supplier?
2. Why is it important to check transport packaging?
3. What happens if the snacks are too oily?
4. How do they check the taste of the snacks?

Vocabulary

Match the words by use of linking lines. Then use them to complete the sentences.

quality	life
inspection	control
shelf	analysis
finished	in
goods	goods
chemical	points

1. All _____ are stored in a warehouse ready for despatch.
2. There are five main _____ in our quality control programme.
3. The _____ department is next to the production hall.
4. The _____ of our ingredients is about two weeks. After that we throw them away.
5. We check all _____ when they arrive at our warehouse.
6. The _____ is carried out in a laboratory in the QC department.

Complete the following sentences with the correct form of the phrases in the box.

break down	cut out	shut down	key in
push through	start up	burn out	turn on

1. We lost productivity on Line Four because the conveyor _broke down_.
2. Don't forget to _____ the date on the labelling machine before you start.
3. The operator overloaded the machine and _____ the motor.
4. We have a safety routine before we _____ the assembly line in the morning.
5. The packaging machine _____ about 12,000 units a day.
6. We've had to _____ Line Three for emergency maintenance work.

7. The motors always _____ when they get too hot.
8. Make sure the power is _____ at the mains supply.

 Task 5 **Look at the notice below. It shows the different divisions of a manufacturing company.**

- For Questions 1–5, decide where each person should go.
- For each question, mark the correct letter a–h.
- Do not use any letter more than once.

a. Production line	e. Quality control
b. Warehouse	f. Packing line
c. Despatch	g. Canteen
d. Research&development	h. Washrooms

1. Sam needs to get changed and freshen up after her shift.
2. Vince wants to research how the goods are currently manufactured.
3. Kate needs to take sample products for inspection.
4. John needs to check the quality of the storage facilities.
5. Ian wants to see what happens to the goods after they have been packed.

Listening

 Task 6 **Brian Benfield talks about production problems at the bakery. Before you listen, decide which of the following would cause problems most often. Then listen and compare your answers.**

- human problems
- electronic problems
- mechanical problems

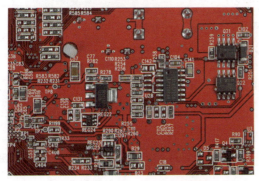

TASK 7 Listen again and complete the sentences.

1. The computer stops the whole process _____.
2. If the computer gets the mix wrong, _____.
3. If a mixerman forgets the yeast and additives, _____.
4. When an old tray loses its shape, _____.
5. We can lose up to an hour and a half of production _____.

Business communication

TASK 8 Work in pairs. Suppose you are going to write an article about quality control at some successful factories in your partner's hometown for a business review. Interview your partner about it and take notes. Start your questions as below.

| Could you tell me a bit about…? | What do they look for…? | |
| What… do they run…? | What do they check for…? | How do they…? |

Translation

TASK 9 Translate the following sentences into Chinese.

1. Next, we inspect all goods in on arrival at our factory and the third inspection point is during production.

2. We take samples to check there isn't too much cooking oil on the snack and that each snack has the minimum amount of flavouring.

3. We check individual bags to make sure that the packet weight is above the acceptable minimum and that the packet is sealed properly.

4. This company develops and delivers a lot of analytical solutions for advanced and innovative processes of quality control.

5. Every step in the production of industrial goods needs continuously monitor to guarantee the quality at all times.

Translate the following sentences into English.

1. 购物网站应当严格检查商户资格并筛选出假冒伪劣商品。（inspect）

2. 你认为一家工厂在质量控制的各个阶段分别需要检查什么？（check for）

3. 股东们对这家公司今年的业绩不太满意，但又不得不接受。（be happy with）

4. 为了延长保质期和促进销售，我们开发了真空包装的豆腐产品。（shelf-life）

5. 这家新公司采取严格的措施以保证每一件产品的包装按要求密封。（seal）

Writing

Suppose you are David Wang. You are writing a letter of application to Company A, applying for the position of Quality Control Manager.

You need to
- tell the addressee how you get the application information;
- introduce briefly your educational background, working experience, skills, etc.;
- make a brief presentation of your knowledge about QC in a company;
- tell the addressee the way of your contact.

Business know-how

Read the following passage and make an oral summary of the main points to your partner or group.

Business plan（商业计划书）

A business plan is a formal statement of business goals, reasons they are attainable, and plans for reaching them. It may also contain background information about the organisation or team attempting to reach those goals. Written business plans are often required to obtain a bank loan or other financing.

Business plans may target changes in perception and branding by the customer, client, taxpayer, or larger community. When the existing business is to assume a major change or when planning a new venture（投机活动；经营项目）, a 3 to 5 years' business plan is required, since investors will look for their investment return in that time frame.

Business plans may be internally or externally focused. Externally focused plans target goals that are important to external stakeholders（参与人，参与方）, particularly financial stakeholders. They typically have detailed information about the organisation or team attempting to reach the goals. With for-profit entities, external stakeholders include investors and customers. External stake holders of non-profits include donors and the clients of the non-profit's services. For government agencies, external stakeholders include taxpayers, higher-level government agencies, and international lending bodies such as the International Monetary Fund, the World Bank, various economic agencies of the United Nations, and development banks.

Internally focused business plans target intermediate goals required to reach the external goals. They may cover the development of a new product, a new service, a new IT system, a restructuring of finance, the refurbishing（再装修）of a factory or a restructuring（重建）of the organisation. An internal business plan is often developed in conjunction with a balanced scorecard（记分卡）or a list of critical success factors. This allows the success of the plan to be measured using non-financial measures. Business plans that identify and target internal goals, but provide only general guidance on how they will be met are called strategic plans.

Text B Improving quality

Mazli is in a meeting with Amrit Singh, the Production Director, and Lu Wei, the Operations Manager.

Amrit OK, so we all know there's a problem with reject levels, but before we look at ways of dealing with it, what I'd like to know is why don't we find the rejects sooner. How can they get all the way to the finished goods chemical analysis before we find them? Lu Wei?

Lu Wei Well, Amrit. The problem is the oil temperature in the cookers. It keeps falling or rising suddenly. And that's why the samples don't always pick up high fat levels. The problem is worse when demand is high and we're running at full capacity, well, like we are at the moment.

Amrit So what can we do about it?

Lu Wei Well, I think the first idea on your memo is the best one. We should increase the sampling rate. You see, if we take samples more often, we'll pick up the rejects sooner.

Mazli That's true, but if we do that, we'll need extra human resources in the QC department. I prefer the second idea. I'd rather just change the temperature sensors in the cookers.

Lu Wei We've already tried that, but it didn't make any difference. The problem is the oil in the cookers. When it gets dirty the temperature sensors don't work properly.

Mazli So why don't we change the oil more often?

Lu Wei Well, it would help, but we have to stop production to change the oil. We're going to lose production capacity if we stop the line more often. And the extra oil will increase our costs, of course.

Amrit Hmm. That's a point.

Mazli Yes, but if it reduces the reject levels, a bit of lost production won't be a problem.

Lu Wei It might not be a problem if we can reduce reject levels to zero, but I don't think that's possible.

Amrit OK. Let's try it anyway. Lu Wei, I'd like you to change the oil more often and monitor the sensors. Mazli, I'd like you to increase the sampling rate by just 10 percent. That means you won't need extra staff. Let's do that for the next two weeks and see what happens. OK?

Mazli Right.

Words and expressions

capacity /kəˈpæsəti/	n. 容量	pick up	获取
reject /ˈriːdʒekt/	n. 次品；不合格品	QC department	质量控制部门
sensor /ˈsensə(r)/	n. 传感器	reject level	不合格水平
make any difference	有任何影响；有任何关系	sampling rate	抽样率

Comprehension tasks

 Read the text and the memo below. Then answer the following questions.

1. What is the problem?
2. What causes it?
3. Which proposals do Lu Wei and Mazli each support?
4. What action does Amrit decide to take?

Alibaba Quality Snacks
Internal Memorandum

To: Mazli Amhar
cc: Lu Wei
From: Amrit Singh
Date: March 8, 2011

Re: QC Meeting   March 9, 2011

Our reject levels have risen by over five percent in three weeks. Chemical analysis shows that fat levels are above the acceptable maximum.

Here are some ideas for dealing with the problem. Please be prepared to discuss them at the meeting.

1 Increase the sampling rate
2 Change the cooker temperature sensors
3 Change the cooking oil more often

Read the text again and choose the best option to complete each sentence.

1. The samples do not pick up the high fat levels because
   a. the cooker does not work properly.
   b. the oil temperature changes too quickly.
   c. the factory is running at full capacity.
2. Mazli does not want to increase the sampling rate because she
   a. thinks the rate is already good enough.
   b. has not got enough staff in her department.
   c. does not think it will make a difference.
3. Lu Wei does not want to change the sensors because
   a. the sensors are very expensive.
   b. it would mean losing production.
   c. he has already changed them.
4. The temperature sensors do not work properly
   a. when the cooker oil gets dirty.
   b. if samples are not taken regularly.
   c. because the cookers are old.
5. Lu Wei does not want to change the oil more often because
   a. it will be expensive and cut production.
   b. he thinks changing sensors is a better idea.
   c. he does not think it will make a difference.

Vocabulary

 Match the words and phrases with their opposites by use of linking lines. Then complete the text with the correct form of the words and phrases. Do not use any of them more than once.

1. demand   fall
2. goods in   increase
3. rise   accept
4. reject   supply
5. reduce   finished goods

The problems started about six months ago. We were already at full capacity when (1) _____ suddenly went up by 30%. We only had one warehouse so both

(2) _____ and (3) _____ were in the same place. There was no way we could (4) _____ our storage space so we worked very closely with our (5) _____ , who delivered the ingredients just when we needed them and not before. On the production side, both workers and machinery had to work overtime and our quality levels began to (6) _____. We soon noticed a(an) (7) _____ in our (8) _____ levels and we had to throw away more and more finished goods. But we couldn't really do anything about it without (9) _____ capacity so we just had to (10) _____ the situation.

 Complete the word diagram with the verbs in the box.

install	weigh	label	repair	inspect	package	mend
despatch	protect	fix	check	prevent	wrap	fasten

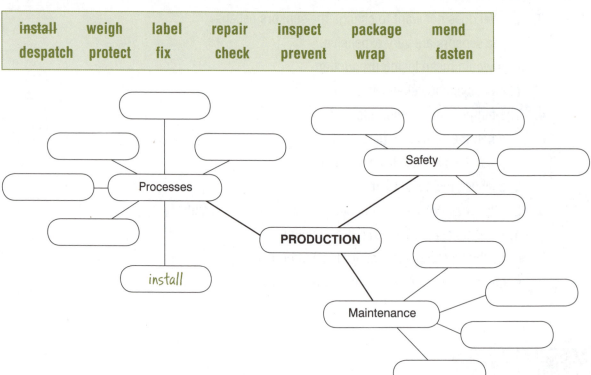

 Complete the email with the words and phrases in the box.

assembly line	component	installation	machine
operators	schedule	overload	adjustments

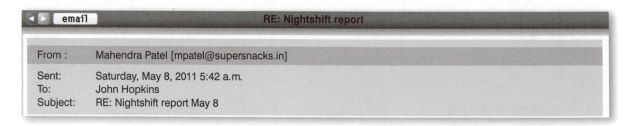

Nightshift report May 8
Shift manager: Ravi Singh

John

We had a few problems with (1) _assembly line_ Number Two—mostly with the packaging (2) _____. Two motors burned out last night. The fitters have just finished the (3) _____ of the new motors. It took a while because they had problems getting a (4) _____. Anyway, they're making some final (5) _____ and then it should be ready.

Could you tell your (6) _____ not to (7) _____ the machines as I think that's causing the problems. If we run the line at a steady 600 units per hour, we should still meet our production (8) _____ for the week.

Have a good shift.

Speaking

TASK 6 Work in pairs. What QC processes are there at a food or beverage manufacturer in China?

TASK 7 Form a pair and discuss the following topic with your partner.

How to ensure that a company consistently maintains quality control standards

Business communication

TASK 8 Suppose you are the director of a small soft drinks producer. You are going to hear descriptions of different problems at your company and possible solutions. Discuss the problems and decide what action to take. Use some of the structures below.

Let's...   Why don't we...?   We should...

Translation

Translate the following sentences into Chinese.

1. We all know there's a problem with reject levels, but before we look at ways of dealing with it, what I'd like to know is why don't we find the rejects sooner.

2. The problem is worse when demand is high and we're running at full capacity, well, like we are at the moment.

3. I'd like you to increase the sampling rate by just 10 percent. That means you won't need extra staff.

4. The quality management was a focus of our work as we have high standards to meet the needs of our customers.

5. The producer's analytical process control solution guarantees the quality of the product.

Translate the following sentences into English.

1. 有了送餐网络平台，消费者可以在此平台上预订快餐，送餐员以最快的速度在餐馆取餐并送至消费者手中。(pick up)

2. 预计需求会加倍增长，我们必须开足马力生产。(at full capacity)

3. 这几项质量控制新举措能否起到作用还没有定论。(make difference)

4. 政府的主要任务是降低通货膨胀的水平。(reduce the level of)

5. 今年服装企业生产成本增加，市场竞争更加激烈。(costs)

Writing

TASK 11 Suppose you are the manager of QC department of a smartphone company. You are going to write a report about several effective measures taken to improve the quality of the products.

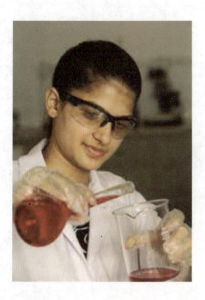

UNIT 4 The call centre

Warming up

  What do you know about call centres? Have you ever thought about working in a call centre? Why or why not?

  Which of the following people would be interested in working in a call centre? Why?

Zoe Connolly, 22

I've just finished university and I'm looking for a job. I've got a degree in business studies but I'm not really sure what I want to do. I'd like to take some time off and travel around the world but I don't have any money.

Vernon Eliot, 32

I'm unemployed at the moment. I've worked in sales a lot and I'd like to continue in that area. I really enjoy working with people and visiting customers. Sales is always interesting because you know you can always sell more, so you never relax.

Marisol Cara, 26

I worked as a secretary after leaving school but I stopped working last year to start a family. My daughter is now nearly six months old and I would like to go back to work. My husband works in an office from nine till five.

Text A — The call centre

Gabe Steele, the National Sales Manager at American Life, talks about call centres.

Journalist American Life was the first direct provider of insurance in the United States when it started twenty-six years ago. Can you tell us a bit about the products you offer?

Gabe Well, most people… when they think about American Life, they think about car insurance. Over the last ten years we've become one of the biggest direct auto insurers in the U.S.A.—and we've recently started to offer a vehicle breakdown service. However, as our name suggests, we were originally best known for our life insurance policies and our home and travel insurance products. We also offer financial services such as mortgages, personal loans, savings and pensions.

Journalist And how many call centres does the company now operate?

Gabe We have 200 regional centres across the United States which employ between 300 and 600 people each. So, in total we have over 100,000 staff in our centres. Almost one in fifty working Americans has some kind of insurance policy with us.

Journalist So what are the advantages of using call centres to buy and sell insurance directly?

Gabe Well, the biggest advantage of direct service is the same for both the company and our customers—we all save money. Direct auto insurance means there is no middleman; consequently the price of the insurance is lower for the client. And the costs are lower for the company because call centres are cheap to run. We don't have to pay high rents for good main street locations or pay commission to brokers and agents. This means we can offer our customers lower premiums.

Journalist OK. And how does a call centre affect the quality of service a customer gets?

Gabe When a customer calls, they get an instant response. The computer database shows all the customer's details, which saves a lot of time. When people say they don't like call centres, they forget how much slower things were in the past. For example, we can now process insurance claims up to three times more quickly. Our call centres allow us to offer our customers much quicker service as well as lower prices.

Journalist So far, American Life hasn't followed the trend of "offshoring" its call centres to locations outside the United States where labour is cheaper and costs are even lower. Is this something that might happen in the future?

Gabe No. And at American Life we don't believe that offshoring is the future for the call centre industry. You see many companies who have off-shored their call centres are not happy with the result. The different language and culture create a lot of problems and isn't always as cheap as they hoped. Labour costs are likely to rise fast in places like India and as the economy develops, companies will probably have difficulty finding and keeping staff. In the future, companies might relocate their call centres back in the States. We've kept our call centres right here and we believe this was the right decision.

Journalist So how do you see the future for call centres?

Gabe I believe virtual call centres are the future. We're starting to use more home-based agents who do the same jobs as our call centre staff but who work from home. That way we can hire new staff from across the whole country instead of in a fifty-mile radius round a call centre. We have a lot more possible candidates to choose from for each new job, so we can find people with just the right skills and experience. We can deliver our staff training online, too. In the future, virtual call centres will possibly replace most of our existing call centres because they offer us a way to keep growing our customer service teams without lots of capital investment.

Words and expressions

breakdown /'breɪkdaʊn/	n.	（车辆）故障	
broker /'brəʊkə(r)/	n.	经纪人；代理人	
claim /kleɪm/	n.	索赔	
commission /kə'mɪʃn/	n.	佣金；手续费	
database /'deɪtəbeɪs/	n.	数据库	
existing /ɪg'zɪstɪŋ/	adj.	现有的，现存的	
financial /faɪ'nænʃəl/	adj.	金融的；财务的	
home-based /'həʊmbeɪst/	adj.	居家的	
investment /ɪn'vestmənt/	n.	投资	
loan /ləʊn/	n.	贷款；借款	
mortgage /'mɔːgɪdʒ/	n.	抵押贷款；按揭	

offshoring /ɒf'ʃɔːrɪŋ/	n.	离岸外包业务	
originally /ə'rɪdʒənəlɪ/	adv.	起初，原来	
pension /'penʃən/	n.	养老金；退休金	
premium /'priːmɪəm/	n.	保险费；附加费	
radius /'reɪdɪəs/	n.	半径；周围	
response /rɪ'spɒns/	n.	回答，答复	
virtual /'vɜːtʃʊəl/	adj.	虚拟的，模拟的	
call centre		呼叫中心；客服中心	
direct provider		直接供应商	
insurance policy		保单，保险单	
in total		总计	

Comprehension tasks

 Read the text and complete the journalist's notes.

Notes: American Life

Products
- Insurance lines: auto insurance (**1**) _____ , home and travel insurance
- Vehicle breakdown service
- Financial services: mortgages, personal (**2**) _____ savings and (**3**) _____

Company statistics
Number of call centres: (**4**) _____
Total number of staff: (**5**) _____

Advantages of call centre service
Lower insurance (**6**) _____ for the client and lower (**7**) _____ for the company. When customers call, they get an immediate (**8**) _____.

Future
Offshoring is not the answer because labour (**9**) _____ are likely to rise in places like India. Call centres will probably find it difficult to find and keep (**10**) _____. Gabe Steele believes that (**11**) _____ call centres are the future—they make it possible for companies to hire new staff from across the (**12**) _____.

 TASK 2 Read the text again and choose the correct option to complete each sentence.

1. Using call centres keeps costs lower because the company does not have to
    a. employ lots of workers.
    b. rent shops or pay commission.
    c. pay for advertising.

2. In the future, American Life
    a. will probably relocate its call centres where labour is cheaper.
    b. might relocate its call centres in India.
    c. won't "offshore" its call centres.

3. American Life is starting to hire new staff
    a. who can work from home.
    b. who can do a wider range of different jobs.
    c. who live within a fifty-mile radius round each call centre.

4. When companies use virtual call centres,
    a. they don't need to hire so many staff.
    b. they have more potential staff to choose from.
    c. they don't need to train staff.

40,000

American Life's motor telesales operators handle around 40,000 incoming calls a day.

Unit 4 The call centre

Vocabulary

TASK 3 Look back to the text. How many words connected with insurance can you find? Now write words which go before the word insurance and words which go after.

```
___auto___                    ___broker___
_____                     _____
_____      Insurance      _____
_____                     _____
```

TASK 4 Match the words with the meanings by use of linking lines.

1. broker — money you pay for insurance
2. premium — person who buys and sells things, e.g. insurance, for other people
3. claim — money paid to a salesperson for every sale he/she makes
4. policy — loan to buy a house
5. mortgage — request for money to be paid by an insurer
6. commission — insurance contract

TASK 5 Match the words by use of linking lines. Then use them to complete the sentences.

financial	bank
insurance	services
exchange	card
fixed	agreement
service	policy
currency	rate
credit	exchange
central	term

1. _Financial services_ has been one of the real growth industries in the last fifteen years.
2. We took out a(an) _____ against fire, flood and storm damage.
3. The U.S. dollar—pound _____ is beginning to cause us concern.
4. I usually put all expenses on a company _____ when travelling on business.
5. We took out a loan for a(an) _____ of ten years.
6. The European _____ has left the base rate on hold again this month.
7. Monthly statements and personal banking are part of our _____.

8. The introduction of the euro should reduce our annual _____ costs.

Listening

TASK 6 Gabe Steele talks about working conditions in a call centre. Listen and complete the following sentences.

1. We sometimes read _____ stories about working conditions in call centres.
2. Yes, the computer system does _____ whether agents are at their desks, but we make sure that they get an hour for lunch and plenty of other breaks.
3. The monitoring affects the agents' pay in a _____ way.
4. Every team also has a _____ whose role it is to support the agents and to help them with difficult or unusual customer enquiries.
5. The computer system works out a shift plan based on the calls it expects and plans _____ the right number of agents for each time of day. So shift times are _____.
6. We also organise fun _____ during big sporting events like the World Cup or the Olympics.

TASK 7 Listen to the recording again and decide whether the following statements are "True" or "False".

1. The computer system monitors the workers every minute of their shift.   True/False
2. Call centre agents can earn productivity bonuses for selling a lot of policies.   True/False
3. Agents normally work a lot more hours than office workers.   True/False
4. Agents work the same hours every month.   True/False
5. The call centre is open from 9 a.m. until 5 p.m. on weekdays.   True/False
6. Call centres employ a lot of young people and women.   True/False
7. The company tries to make working in the call centre more interesting.   True/False

Business communication

TASK 8 Work in pairs. Call centres are a growing business sector across the world. Why do you think companies invest so much money in them?

Translation

 Translate the following sentences into Chinese.

1. Over the last ten years we've become one of the biggest direct auto insurers in the U.S.A.—and we've recently started to offer a vehicle breakdown service.

2. We don't have to pay high rents for good main street locations or pay commission to brokers and agents.

3. In the future, virtual call centres will possibly replace most of our existing call centres because they offer us a way to keep growing our customer service teams without lots of capital investment.

4. For the past 10 years, countries such as China have been exporting capital to the U.S. and the U.K. so that we have lived beyond our means.

5. One of the most important changes is the investment of pension.

 Translate the following sentences into English.

1. 建议阅读家庭财产和汽车保险单中的附属细则。(insurance policy)

2. 在为意外事故、疾病与失业投保之前一定要考虑清楚。(insure)

3. 他办理过失业保险，可是当他去索赔时却遭拒付。(claim)

4. 中国经济有较大可能在 2020 年前保持 8% 的年均增速。(be likely to)

5. 几千名领取养老金的人被劝说用自己的住房作抵押去投资投机性债券。(mortgage, invest)

Writing

 Write down your ideas about what call centres will be like in the future. Try to talk about possibility as suggested in the following examples.

You may write from the following aspects:
- How is the working environment?
- What is the working mechanism?
- What are the advantages and disadvantages compared with today's call centres?

Business know-how

Read the following passage and make an oral summary of the main points to your partner or group.

Insurance（保险）

Insurance is a means of protection against financial loss. It is a form of risk management, and primarily used to hedge against（避免损失）the risk of a contingent（或有的，不确定的）or uncertain loss.

An entity which provides insurance is known as an insurer, insurance company, insurance carrier or underwriter. A person or entity who buys insurance is known as an insured or as a policyholder. The insurance transaction involves the insured assuming a guaranteed and known relatively small loss in the form of payment to the insurer in exchange for the insurer's promise to compensate（补偿，赔偿）the insured in the event of a covered loss. The loss may or may not be financial, but it must be reducible to financial terms, and usually involves something in which the insured has an insurable interest established by ownership, possession, or preexisting relationship.

The insured receives a contract, called the insurance policy, which details the conditions and circumstances under which the insurer will compensate the insured. The amount of money charged by the insurer to the insured for the coverage set forth in the insurance policy is called the premium（保险费）. If the insured experiences a loss which is potentially covered by the insurance policy, the insured submits a claim to the insurer for processing by a claims adjuster. The insurer may hedge its own risk by taking out reinsurance, whereby another insurance company agrees to carry some of the risk, especially if the primary insurer deems that the risk is too large for it to carry.

Text B Call centre creates 2,000 jobs in the Philippines

HJC Bank is setting up a call centre in Boracay in the central Philippines because of the growth of its Internet and telephone banking service. This is a welcome decision for the area, which companies considered less attractive than regions such as India, Malaysia or Singapore in their list of the best locations for call centres. Opening early next year, the centre is expected to employ 2,000 people over the next three years.

HJC Bank, the Internet and telephone banking service, was introduced in 2010 and has more than 600,000 customers. The service is helped by the well-developed telecoms infrastructure of the Philippines and the high standard of English. HJC Bank is attracting 25,000 new customers every month and the bank expects one million customers over the next two years. One director said: "Opening another call centre shows how popular our Internet and telephone banking service is with our customers. HJC Bank will continue to invest to satisfy their needs."

Words and expressions

attractive	/əˈtræktɪv/	adj. 有吸引力的	well-developed	/ˈweldɪˈveləpt/	adj. 发展良好的
infrastructure	/ˈɪnfrəstrʌktʃə(r)/	n. 基础设施	banking service		银行服务
introduce	/ˌɪntrəˈdjuːs/	v. 引进	be expected to		有望；应该
satisfy	/ˈsætɪsfaɪ/	v. 使满意；使满足	be popular with		受……欢迎

Comprehension tasks

Read the text and answer the following questions.

1. Why is HJC Bank setting up a call centre in Boracay in the central Philippines?
2. What are the companies' opinion about this area?
3. When was HJC Bank introduced and how could it make it possible to provide its Internet and telephone banking service?

Read the text again and circle "True" or "False". Correct the false sentences.

1. The call centre that HJC Bank is setting up will open early this year and 20,000 people are expected to be employed over the next three years. True/False
2. Introduced in 2010, HJC Bank provides the Internet and telephone banking service for over 600,000 customers. True/False
3. Every year, HJC Bank is attracting 25,000 new customers and now its customers are reaching almost one million. True/False

Vocabulary

 Which word is the odd one out?

1. contract   policy   agreement   memorandum
2. cost   claim   premium   price
3. premium   location   price   commission
4. instant   immediate   exciting   fast
5. life   loan   auto   house
6. volume   total   quality   number
7. loan   mortgage   provider   pension

 Complete the following sentences with the words in the box.

| supervisor | loan | premium | monitor | policy |
| commission | claim | broker | enquiry | |

1. I changed my car insurance because the _____ was lower.
2. I bought the car with a(an) _____ from the bank.
3. We know a(an) _____ who advises us on insurance.
4. As an insurance salesman he earns _____ on everything he sells.
5. A new customer phoned me to make a(an) _____.
6. The system lets us _____ what the operatives are doing at any time.
7. My car has just been stolen so I need to make a(an) _____.
8. Her house insurance _____ ran out last month.
9. A(An) _____ makes decisions if operatives have to deal with large or unusual risks.

Match the multi-word verbs with the nouns by use of linking lines.

1. insure against — debt/difficulties
2. sort out — fire/loss
3. fill in — shares/a company
4. invest in — a claims form/an application
5. get into — a problem/a disagreement

Speaking

Work in pairs. Are the following situations likely in your country?

1. Customer-service companies will outsource and offshore almost all their business.
2. Automated customer services systems with "virtual" agents will completely replace people.
3. Call centres will use video-phones for face-to-face contact.

Form a pair and discuss the following topic with your partner.

Have you ever called a call centre? Did you get a satisfactory answer?

Business communication

More and more organisations sell their services and products directly to customers online. Work in pairs and discuss the following questions.

- What are the advantages and disadvantages of the Internet business model a) for customers and b) for a business?
- What kinds of business is it not appropriate for?

Translation

Translate the following sentences into Chinese.

1. HJC Bank is setting up a call centre in Boracay in the central Philippines because of the growth of its Internet and telephone banking service.

2. This is a welcome decision for the area, which companies considered less attractive than regions such as India, Malaysia or Singapore in their list of the best locations for call centres.

3. HJC Bank, the Internet and telephone banking service, was introduced in 2010 and has more than 600,000 customers.

4. Difficult changes have been introduced by the government to transit to a market economy.

5. Central banks do not provide a full banking service for personal and commercial customers.

Translate the following sentences into English.

1. 我们不仅把客户看作是消费者，我们还把他们当作朋友。(consider)

2. 经济不景气时，消费者可能会减少在类似玩具等非必需品上的支出。(be expected to)

3. 这家公司从国外引进了新的生产机器。(introduce)

4. 这个产品会受年轻消费者的欢迎。(be popular with)

5. 美国和一些欧洲国家有着良好的保险和养老金制度，为退休人口提供经济支持。(well-developed)

Writing

TASK 11 Think about the questions in Task 8 carefully and write down your answers with well-organised language and well-arranged structure.

Part I Listening comprehension

TASK 1 Listen to Starbucks and Uber CEOs talking to CNBC. Fill in each blank with the missing information. You will hear the talk TWICE.

1. CEO of Starbucks said that Starbucks Delivery in United States is in _____ with UberEats.
2. It was said that a small _____ from Starbucks and from Uber cooperated into developing software.
3. It is a fact that more customers are embracing the _____. They want personal life experiences, and they want more channels to order and to get their favourite food and beverage.
4. Technology used to be just something in the digital world, but it is now getting more and more into the _____.
5. CEO of Uber felt amazed about working with Starbucks in that their goal of transforming the _____ is incredible.

TASK 2 Listen to the eight short recordings and choose the correct answers. You will hear each recording TWICE.

1. What does Alison order?
   a. Fish.   b. Steak.   c. Chicken.
2. Which is the flight to Sydney?

LH4521	LH4152	LH4125
a	b	c

3. Which hotel does Graham's colleague recommend?
   a. The Orion.   b. The Grand Hotel.   c. The Plaza.
4. Which machine are the people talking about?
   a. A fax machine.   b. A printer.   c. A photocopier.
5. What happens to the phone call?
   a. The receptionist puts the caller through.
   b. The receptionist takes a message.
   c. The caller offers to ring back later.
6. How much does the retailer pay for each game?
   a. $7 a unit.   b. $8 a unit.   c. $9 a unit.
7. How long will the order take to arrive?
   a. Three days.   b. Four days.   c. Five days.

8. What is wrong with the printer?
   a. It has run out of paper.
   b. The paper has jammed.
   c. It needs a new ink cartridge.

TASK 3 Listen to a news broadcast and answer the following questions. You will hear the news TWICE.

1. Why did the Chilean businessman say that doing business in China has become easier?
2. Why did the Chilean businessman have reason to be optimistic?
3. What are the four international events hosted by China this year where Xi reaffirmed the commitment in speeches delivered?

Part II Reading and writing

TASK 4 Look at the graphs below. They show unemployment in eight different regions compared to the national average. Which region does each sentence describe? For each sentence mark the correct letter. Do not use any letter more than once.

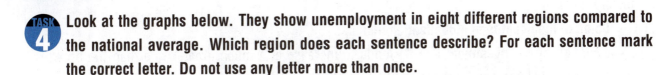

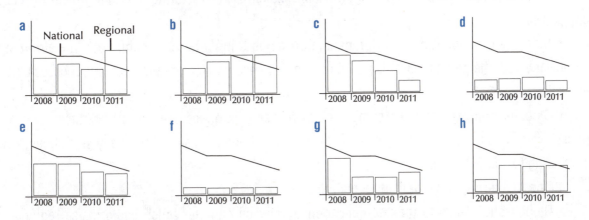

1. After an initial fall, unemployment figures remained steady before showing a slight increase, in contrast to the national situation.
2. Unemployment fell steadily throughout the period and remained below the national average.
3. Despite a drop in the national average, the rate of unemployment remained steady for two years before falling in 2010.
4. Although there was a fall in the national average, unemployment in this region rose sharply at the end of the period.
5. After rising steadily, unemployment finally began to reflect the national situation and decreased.

TASK 5 Read the following passage quickly and decide whether each of the following statements is "True" or "False".

The impact of globalisation on economic growth

By Justin Kuepper, Updated November 19, 2018

Globalisation has impacted nearly every aspect of modern life. Most economists agree that globalisation provides a net benefit to individual economies around the world, by making markets more efficient, increasing competition, limiting military conflicts, and spreading wealth more equally around the world.

However, the general public tends to assume that the costs associated with globalisation outweigh the benefits, especially in the short term.

But, in aggregate, there is a consensus among economists that globalisation provides a net benefit to nations around the world and therefore should be embraced on the whole by governments and individuals.

Some of the benefits of globalisation include:

• Foreign direct investment ("FDI") tends to increase at a much greater rate than the growth in world trade, helping boost technology transfer, industrial restructuring, and the growth of global companies.

• Increased competition from globalisation helps stimulate new technology development, particularly with the growth in FDI, which helps improve economic output by making processes more efficient.

• Globalisation enables large companies to realise economies of scale that reduce costs and prices, which in turn supports further economic growth, although this can hurt many small businesses attempting to compete domestically.

Some of the risks of globalisation include:

• Globalisation leads to the interdependence between nations, which could cause regional or global instabilities if local economic fluctuations end up impacting a large number of countries relying on them.

• Some see the rise of nation-states, multinational or global firms and other international organisations as a threat to sovereignty. Ultimately, this could cause some leaders to become nationalistic.

• The benefits of globalisation can be unfairly skewed towards rich nations or individuals, creating greater inequalities and leading to potential conflicts both nationally and internationally as a result.

1. Most economists argue that globalisation benefits world economy in general.　　True/False
2. In the long run, globalisation brings more costs to people's life.　　True/False

3. Economists encourage governments and individuals to welcome globalisation.   True/False
4. Globalisation brings the same cost reduction benefits to both small and large businesses.   True/False
5. Fierce competition among businesses increased by globalisation helps improve productivity.   True/False
6. Local economic changes seldom affect other nations.   True/False
7. Globalisation widens the gap between rich nations and poor nations.   True/False

Read the email and the information about theatre performances and complete the form below.

To: jane.little@Abstrakt.com
From: enrique.garcia@Abstrakt.com
Subject: Theatre tickets

Epcom visit on Friday

Could you book some theatre tickets for tomorrow for the five Epcom visitors and me? We'll be in a meeting all day until about 4:30 p.m. and then we'll have an early dinner together at the hotel. Could you phone the ticket agency and find a play or something that starts after half past seven p.m.? Use the company VISA card to pay for the tickets.

Enrique

What's on: Theatre

Hamlet at the Barbican.
Performances start at 19:15.
Tickets £17.50–£75

West Side Story at the Play house.
Show starts at 19:00.
Tickets £15.50–£80

Buddy Holly at the Palace Theatre.
Performances at 15:30 and 20:00.
Tickets £16.50–£65

BOOKING
Name of show: (1) _____
Venue: (2) _____
Method of payment: (3) _____
Time: (4) _____
No. of tickets: (5) _____

Suppose your company has planned for a new product launch. You are in charge of presenting a new electronic gadget. Write a presentation that includes the following information:

- the features and functions of the product;
- the place of the product launch;
- the price of the product.

Part III Business knowledge and translation

Briefly define the following underlined business terms in English and translate each term into Chinese.

1. Proper product development ensures that the end product support all requirements while meeting all codes required of particular type of product.
   Definition: _____
   Translation: _____

2. You must always follow quality control guidelines so that you know your business is doing things in the right way.
   Definition: _____
   Translation: _____

3. As a means to stave off bankruptcy, the board had decided that offshoring jobs to another country would be the only way to save the company.
   Definition: _____
   Translation: _____

4. Making a big capital investment can be a risky proposition but may also pay off big for you or your company.
   Definition: _____
   Translation: _____

5. You need to have a great distribution team, so that your product can arrive to its customers on time.
   Definition: _____
   Translation: _____

Translate the following Chinese passage into English.

当我回顾2017年，毫无疑问，通用电气度过了非常艰难的一年。收益下降了1%，达到1 221亿美元，通过股息和回购，通用电气向投资者返还了121亿美元。许多人对我们失去了信心，我没有。对于每一个与通用电气相关的人来说，这也是一个反思公司的意义和它存在的原因的机会。我们的技术解决了世界上最棘手的问题。我们为180多个国家的客户而奋斗并为其提供支持。

UNIT 5 Banking

Warming up

 Discuss with your partner what changes you find in banking sector.

 Match the jobs with the duties by use of linking lines.

1. bank clerk
2. lawyer
3. personal banker
4. investment banker
5. insurance broker
6. legal secretary
7. claims assessor
8. courier

a. represents a company in court/gives legal advice
b. cashes cheques/exchanges currency/gives balances
c. transports documents and parcels quickly
d. sells policies/advises clients/assesses risk
e. advises companies on buying stocks and shares
f. assists lawyers/does research and general office duties
g. advises on account management/sells banking products
h. decides on the level of insurance payouts

Text A Internet banking

Denise Le Blanc enquires about Internet banking.

Clerk   Hello. Can I help you?
Denise Yes, I'd like some information on your Internet banking service.
Clerk   Certainly. Do you have an account with us?
Denise Yes, I do. This is my home branch.
Clerk   Well, with our Internet banking service you can do all your day-to-day banking online at any time of day or night.
Denise How does it work?
Clerk   All you do is log in, key in your PIN number, choose the service you want and then just follow the instructions. It's as easy as that.
Denise And what can I actually do online?

Clerk You can check your balance, pay bills, order a statement or transfer money. All your normal day-to-day banking.
Denise Does it cost anything?
Clerk No. The service is part of your normal bank account.
Denise Oh, right. And can I log in at any time of the day?
Clerk Yes, you can. The service is available 24 hours-a-day, seven days a week.
Denise Could I fill in a form now?
Clerk Certainly. One moment, I'll just get an application form…

Words and expressions

application	/ˌæplɪˈkeɪʃən/	n.	申请	statement	/ˈsteɪtmənt/	n.	结算表；财务报表
clerk	/klɜːk/	n.	职员	transfer	/trænsˈfɜː(r)/	v.	转移；转账
day-to-day	/ˈdeɪtuːdeɪ/	adj.	日常的	key in			输入
instruction	/ɪnˈstrʌkʃən/	n.	指示；说明	log in			注册

Comprehension tasks

 Denise Le Blanc has noted down some questions. Read the text again and answer the questions.

Vocabulary

Match the verbs with the nouns by use of linking lines.

1. check   bills
2. transfer   a balance
3. pay   a form
4. order   a PIN number
5. sign   a statement
6. follow   money
7. key in   instructions

Complete the following sentences with the correct gerunds in the box.

| advising | borrowing | insuring | lending | repaying | withdrawing |

1. We've started ___advising___ all our U.K. customers to quote prices in dollars.
2. The bank continued _____ them money despite their heavy debts.
3. We're trying to avoid _____ too much money from our company account.
4. They suggested _____ money from private investors to finance our plan.
5. We should think about _____ all our data against fire or theft.
6. We should finish _____ the loan by the end of the year.

Choose the correct word to complete each sentence.

1. The average credit card *debit/debt* in the U.K. is around £2,000.
2. We had to *borrow/lend* money from the bank to finance the expansion.
3. The "creditors" section of a balance sheet shows what a company *owes/debts*.
4. The company gets a monthly *settlement/statement* from the bank.
5. The bank gets 1% currency exchange *surcharge/commission* on foreign transfers.
6. Most customers nowadays *deposit/withdraw* money from cash machines.
7. We took out a *loan/credit* with a 4% interest rate.
8. Our biggest single cost is the *hire/rent* we pay on our premises.

TASK 5 Complete the table. Then use the words in the right form to complete the sentences.

Verb	Noun
solve	solution
claim	_____
_____	repayment
insure	_____
_____	collection
support	_____
_____	advice
settle	_____

1. Banks are often an expensive __solution__ to the problem of raising capital.
2. We asked our _____ broker to find us the cheapest policy he could.
3. The bank provided financial _____ during our cash flow problems.
4. Our legal department _____ us on all copyright issues.
5. After all the floods, they processed our _____ very quickly.
6. Any debt unpaid for twelve months is transferred to a debt _____ agency.
7. We received a cheque to _____ the outstanding balance of the account.
8. The monthly _____ on the loan should finish in about three months' time.

Listening

TASK 6 Denise applies for the Internet banking service. Listen and answer the following questions.

1. Did Denise register successfully?
2. How will Denise get membership number?

Listen again and complete the form.

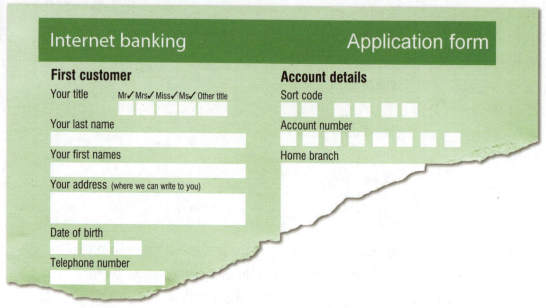

Business communication

 Work in pairs. Suppose you are a customer who wants to open a bank account and your partner is a bank clerk. Please make a conversation about the application process.

Translation

 Translate the following sentences into Chinese.

1. With our Internet banking service you can do all your day-to-day banking online at any time of day or night.

2. All you do is log in, key in your PIN number, choose the service you want and then just follow the instructions.

3. You can check your balance, pay bills, order a statement or transfer money.

4. Making the central bank independent was one of Brown's greatest achievements: he has no day-to-day control over it.

5. Customers need to make sure they have sufficient funds in their account before they spend.

 Translate the following sentences into English.

1. 人们可以通过网上银行随时随地进行转账。(transfer)

2. 账户申请表可从银行网页下载。(available)

3. 申请银行账户需要填写个人信息。(fill in)

4. 银行会每月按时给客户发送结算单。(statement)

5. 在进行网上交易时需要仔细确认信息。(check)

Writing

 Write an article about the advantages and disadvantages of e-banking.

Business know-how

Read the following passage and make an oral summary of the main points to your partner or group.

Banking history（银行业的历史）

Modern banking practices, including fractional reserve banking（部分准备金银行制度）and the issue of banknotes, emerged in the 17th and 18th centuries. Merchants started to store their gold with the goldsmiths of London, who possessed private vaults (保险库，金库), and charged a fee for that service. In exchange for each deposit of precious metal, the goldsmiths issued receipts certifying the quantity and purity of the metal they held as a bailee (受委托人); these receipts could not be assigned; only the original depositor could collect the stored goods.

Gradually the goldsmiths began to lend the money out on behalf of the depositor, which led to the development of modern banking practices; promissory notes (which evolved into banknotes) were issued for money deposited as a loan to the goldsmiths. The goldsmiths paid interest on these deposits. Since the promissory notes were payable on demand, and the advances (loans) to the goldsmiths' customers were repayable over a longer time period, this was an early form of fractional reserve banking. The promissory notes developed into an assignable instrument which could circulate as a safe and convenient form of money backed by the goldsmiths' promise to pay, allowing goldsmiths to advance loans with little risk of default (违约). Thus, the goldsmiths of London became the forerunners of banking by creating new money based on credit.

Text B The banking revolution

The new face of banking in the 21st century

Twenty years on from the banking revolution

The banking revolution of the last two decades has caused huge changes in the way that banks conduct their businesses and interact with their customers; but what are the results of these changes in real terms? Are bank customers getting a better service, and are the banks themselves more efficient?

The three C's

Martha Hogan, head of customer relations at YourBank, believes the answer is "yes". "Customers are delighted they don't have to stand in long queues at the bank anymore. Now they can check their bank balance without leaving the house. But, most importantly, Internet banking puts the customer in complete control. We see it as a good thing that our customers depend on us less. They can use the computer to control their money and to manage it directly." Hogan talks about "The Three C's—control, comfort and convenience". As online banking becomes more developed, customers can choose to do their banking on the move. Nowadays you can use your mobile phone to pay your electricity bill on the train on the way home from work.

The question of customer service

So, is the banking revolution all good news? Not all bank customers think so. Banks invested heavily in developing new technology to create their Internet banking systems and this led to cost-cutting in other areas. Many banks cut thousands of jobs and closed smaller branches to save money. Setting up call centres to service hundreds of branches from just a few locations made it possible to reduce staff numbers even more. However, there are customers that say they still prefer direct contact with their local branch, even if this is only possible during business hours. Whilst the banks are making record profits, many customers believe they are getting a poorer service.

Paperless billing—always a good thing?

It's not just customer service that is a problem. Some customers who changed to paying all their bills online are now changing back. They feel they actually have less control with online billing than paper bills. "Electronic bills don't always contain all the information I need," says Bill Snowdon, who cancelled his "paperless billing" service last month. "Whenever I want to find out information and see my account, it's always very complicated and takes a long time. If online banking does save money for the banks, they should pass this benefit on to the customers by improving their services."

Words and expressions

account /əˈkaʊnt/	n.	账户
bill /bɪl/	n.	账单
branch /brɑːntʃ/	n.	分支；分店
complicated /ˈkɒmplɪkeɪtɪd/	adj.	复杂的
convenience /kənˈviːnɪəns/	n.	便利
cost-cutting /ˈkɒstkʌtɪŋ/	n.	削减成本
delighted /dɪˈlaɪtɪd/	adj.	高兴的
interact /ˌɪntərˈækt/	v.	交流
queue /kjuː/	n.	队列
revolution /ˌrevəˈluːʃən/	n.	革命
bank balance		账户余额
electricity bill		电费单
paperless billing		无纸化账单

Comprehension tasks

 Read the text again and choose the correct option for each question.

1. Martha Hogan thinks Internet banking gives customers more control because
   a. paperless billing saves them money.
   b. they don't rely on the banks so much to manage their money.
   c. they don't have to stand in queues at the bank any more.
2. At the beginning of the banking revolution, banks had to cut staff costs
   a. so they could pay for better IT.
   b. so they could open more call centres.
   c. so they could increase customer service in the smaller branches.
3. Why don't some bank customers like call centres?
   a. Because they don't have enough staff.
   b. Because they can't see the people they are talking to.
   c. Because they can never speak directly to their own branch.
4. How are the banks performing?
   a. They are making more money than ever before.
   b. The cost of IT investment has reduced profits.
   c. They have lost customers and lost money.

 Read the text again and circle "True" or "False". Correct the false sentences.

1. The head of customer relations at YourBank believes the banking revolution can make bank more efficient. True/False
2. Customers depend on the bank more. True/False
3. Banks invested a lot to create their internet banking systems which can cut expenses in other areas. True/False
4. Customers feel that they can have more control with online billing than paper billings. True/False
5. Banks improved their services by online banking. True/False

Vocabulary

Complete the table with the correct verb or noun.

Verb	Noun
merge	_____
_____	increase
Invest	_____
_____	cut
reduce	_____
_____	closure
compete	_____
_____	development

Match the words to make phrases by use of linking lines.

1. compete — in — a service
2. deal — with — a form
3. invest — down — another company
4. pay — in — some details
5. fill — for — problems
6. note — with — new technology

Complete the following website extract with the words in the box.

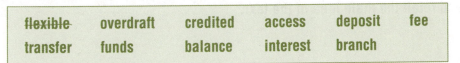

flexible overdraft credited access deposit fee
transfer funds balance interest branch

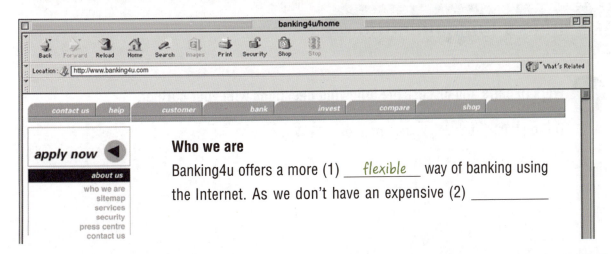

Who we are

Banking4u offers a more (1) ___*flexible*___ way of banking using the Internet. As we don't have an expensive (2) _____ network to maintain, we are able to offer customers unbeatable (3) _____ on their savings. Our new EasyAccess account currently pays 5.45%. With our secure Internet site you can (4) _____ money easily from one account to another at any time and with absolute peace of mind. What's more, any money you send will be (5) _____ to the recipient's account instantly and if the recipient is also a banking4u customer, there'll be no (6) _____ .

Customers also receive a debit card for convenient (7) _____ to their account when shopping. As the banking4u solution is based on a(an) (8) _____ account only, we are currently unable to offer customers a(an) (9) _____ facility. Therefore, customers will need to make sure they have sufficient (10) _____ in their account before they spend. Customers can check their (11) _____ at any time online.

Speaking

Task 6 Work in pairs. Discuss the following questions with your partner.

Do you use any of Internet banking services? What other services would you like?

Task 7 Find a partner and retell the main idea of the text.

Business communication

Task 8 Work in pairs and discuss the following questions with your partner.

Do you think e-banking is important or not? Why?

Translation

 Translate the following sentences into Chinese.

1. The banking revolution of the last two decades has caused huge changes in the way that banks conduct their business and interact with their customers.

2. As online banking becomes more developed, customers can choose to do their banking on the move.

3. Banks invested heavily in developing new technology to create their Internet banking systems and this led to cost-cutting in other areas.

4. Online banking gives you round the clock access to your accounts and let you perform banking functions wherever you are.

5. More and more people are ditching traditional banks and moving to online banks, so they can bank exclusively on their mobile phones or computers.

 Translate the following sentences into English.

1. 科技革命促进了社会各行各业的快速发展。(revolution)

2. 银行的工作人员不断提高工作效率，客户十分满意。(efficient)

3. 电子银行的出现使人们的生活更加方便。(convenience)

4. 银行的手机客户端十分普及，客户可以随时随地查看账户余额。(bank balance)

5. 中国工商银行是中国最大的银行之一，它在全国各地都有分行。(branch)

Writing

 Many banks have their apps. Have you ever used any bank app? And what's your opinion about these apps?

UNIT 6 Trading

Warming up

 TASK 1 What do you think an agent does? And what are the advantages of using an agent?

 TASK 2 Look at the checklist below. It shows the documents which are needed to export machinery.

- For Questions 1–5, decide which documents the people are talking about.
- For each question, mark the correct letter.
- Do not use any letter more than once.

a. Shipping papers	e. Handbook
b. Drawings	f. Parts list
c. Invoice	g. Registration form
d. Specifications	h. Guarantee

1. Two percent discount if payment is within ten days.
2. The customer fills it in and returns it in order to go on our customer mailing list.
3. If they aren't correct, the machine won't get through customs.
4. It's translated so the engineers know how to operate the machine properly.
5. We normally mark on it the spares that we think the customer should always keep in stock.

Text A An import agent

Krallpack GmbH is a small company based near Düsseldorf. The following is the conversation between Joachim Krall, the Managing Director and the journalist.

Journalist Could you tell me about Krallpack and its activities?

Krall We're an agent for Korean manufacturers of packing machinery. We provide them with a European sales network and translate their documents, specifications and parts lists into

	English and other European languages, as required. We also deal with the British customers and all their enquiries and correspondence. And we arrange customers' visits to Korea.
Journalist	Mm, that's very interesting. How did this company begin?
Krall	Before I started Krallpack, I worked in sales for eight years for an international company here in Germany. We had to use some small suppliers of packing machinery to complete our product range. But working with both large and small suppliers caused problems. The smaller companies wanted someone to sell only their products, so in 1992 I left and set up my own company, Krallpack GmbH.
Journalist	That was a big step. And how has this company developed since then?
Krall	Well, I began selling to the drinks industry. Our suppliers began developing excellent new machines that were technically more advanced than our competitors'. These machines helped us to expand into the food and pharmaceutical industries. And our sales people were very good at understanding and selling these new machines so Krallpack got a name for delivering excellent products and providing a service that was fair to both customers and suppliers. Since then turnover has grown to nearly £10m a year and our customers now include companies such as GlaxoSmithKline, Bayer Schering, Rhône-Poulenc and Merck. We moved into these new offices last year and at the moment we're looking for new staff to help the company grow further.
Journalist	Very good. And the future? How do you see the future?
Krall	I think technical development is the key to the industry. Companies have to produce and pack more and more specialised goods to satisfy their customers. So, in future, our suppliers will have to develop their machines technically but without losing any reliability. Our job, of course, is going to be to sell these new machines and continue to provide the best possible support for both our customers and our suppliers.

Words and expressions

agent	/ˈeɪdʒənt/	n.	代理商	**specification**	/ˌspesɪfɪˈkeɪʃən/ n.	产品规格
correspondence	/ˌkɒrəˈspɒndəns/	n.	来往信件	**turnover**	/ˈtɜːnəʊvə(r)/ n.	营业额；成交量
deliver	/dɪˈlɪvə(r)/	v.	递送	**packing machinery**		包装器械
specialised	/ˈspeʃəlaɪzd/	adj.	专业的			

Comprehension tasks

 Read the text and choose the correct option to complete each sentence.

1. Joachim Krall left his job in 1992 because
   a. he did not like the company.
   b. he saw a good business opportunity.
   c. the company had financial problems.
2. Krallpack expanded because
   a. its suppliers built very good machines.
   b. the whole market grew very quickly.
   c. its prices were very low.
3. Krallpack became known for the
   a. fair prices of its products.
   b. quality of its products and service.
   c. skill of its sales people.
4. Krallpack's suppliers will have to develop
   a. their machines and customer support services.
   b. reliable and low priced machines.
   c. technically advanced and reliable machines.

Read the text again and complete the fact file.

Krallpack — FACT FILE

Company Krallpack GmbH
Activities Agent for Korean packing machine manufacturers.
Services
- Provides European sales network.
- (1) _____ documents, specifications and (2) _____ lists.
- Deals with customer enquiries and (3) _____.
- Arranges (4) _____.

Founded In (5) _____.
Customers Major companies include GlaxoSmithKline, Bayer Schering, Rhône-Poulenc and (6) _____.

Vocabulary

 Read the text again and find the nouns that go with the verbs below.

1. deal with — customers / _____ / _____

2. translate — _____ / _____ / _____

3. provide — _____ / _____

TASK 4 Choose the correct option to complete each sentence.

1. Get an engineer in to _____ the machine and get it running again.
   a. mend   b. fasten   c. construct
2. It's too big. It won't _____ into the container.
   a. package   b. install   c. fit
3. Last year the port of Rotterdam was Europe's busiest _____.
   a. dock   b. terminal   c. harbour
4. I returned the goods and asked them to _____ my money.
   a. reward   b. replace   c. refund
5. The goods are _____ in protective film before going to the warehouse.
   a. combined   b. repaired   c. wrapped

TASK 5 Complete the following sentences with the phrases in the box.

| calculate prices | ban imports | list the contents | recycle packaging |
| load the containers | export goods | cross the border | include delivery |

1. Don't forget that when we _calculate prices_, we always have to include import tax and a handling fee for payments.
2. The government is trying to _____ to protect domestic manufacturers from a flood of cheap foreign competition.
3. All the quoted prices are ex works and do not _____ or VAT.
4. It's safer for a company to _____ to its overseas markets than it is to invest large amounts of money in setting up production facilities locally.
5. They managed to _____ on board two hours before the ship left Hamburg.
6. Make sure you _____ on this page of the shipping documents.
7. To reduce waste, we always try to _____ from the deliveries we receive from our own suppliers.
8. The drivers had to wait twelve hours before they were finally allowed to _____ into Slovenia.

Listening

TASK 6 Look at the form below. You will hear a woman checking details about a job advertisement. Write one or two words or a number in the numbered spaces. You will hear the conversation TWICE.

> Computer hardware wholesaler requires a (1) _____ for immediate employment.
> (2) _____ + full benefits.
> Applicants should include full CV, references and details of (3) _____.
> Interviews to be held in the week starting (4) _____.
> Closing date for applications 17 March.

TASK 7 Listen to the passage and fill in the following blanks.

1. Two things are used to describe E.U.-China relations: (1) the two sides do not have _____, which remains true today; (2) _____, which is no longer true.

2. China is the E.U.'s _____. In 2017, _____, a signature of the Belt and Road Initiative ran 1,000 times, a sharp increase of 158 percent on the year before.

3. Every week, around 30 Chinese trains arrive at _____ in Duisburg's inland port in Germany. Their containers are filled with clothes, toys and _____ from Chongqing, Wuhan in Hubei province, or Yiwu in Zhejiang Province, or the trains carry German cars, Scottish whisky, French wine and _____ from Milan the other way.

Business communication

 Work in pairs. Look at the following cards and describe how a customer orders parts through Krallpack. Read the cards and put the process into the correct order.

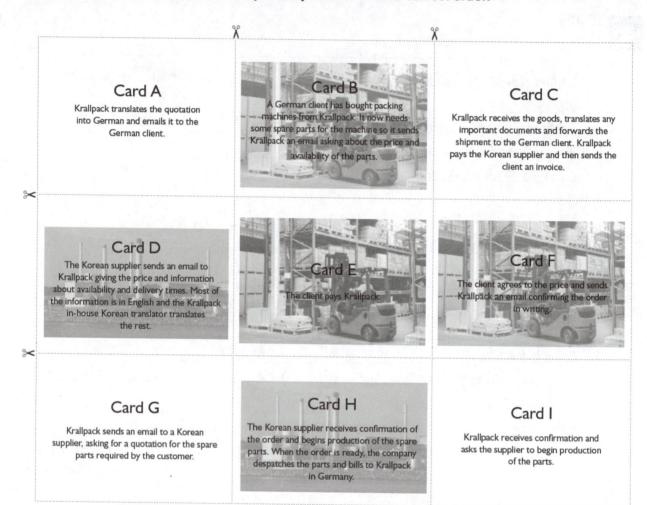

Translation

 Translate the following sentences into Chinese.

1. We provide them with a European sales network and translate their documents, specifications and parts lists into English and other European languages, as required.

2. Our suppliers began developing excellent new machines that were technically more advanced than our competitors'.

3. And our sales people were very good at understanding and selling these new machines so Krallpack got a name for delivering excellent products and providing a service that was fair to both customers and suppliers.

4. Globalisation has been the key of success for many entrepreneurs that decided to sell their products abroad. We believe in expanding businesses worldwide by keeping the costs down minimum.

5. From initial product inquiry to final delivery of goods, MVP Trading offers over 20 years of experience in domestic and international distribution, and exceptional service in English, Russian, and French.

Translate the following sentences into English.

1. 在客户的询盘过程中，了解产品的情况是客户最迫切的要求。(enquiry)

2. 我们公司负责处理客户商务咨询、反馈，整理并形成报告。(deal with)

3. 他创立的公司已在全国建立了分支机构。(set up)

4. 这些工具有助于您提高工作效率，以便按时交付产品，并帮助您应对需求的变化。(deliver)

5. "满足客户的需求"是公司秉承的服务宗旨，"可靠的质量"是公司一贯的追求。(satisfy)

Writing

Suppose you have bought packing machines from Krallpack. You now need some spare parts for the machines. Write an email to Krallpack asking about the price and availability of the parts.

Business know-how

Read the following passage and make an oral summary of the main points to your partner or group.

Trade balance（贸易差额）

The balance of trade forms part of the current account, which includes other transactions（交易）such as income from the net international investment position as well as international aid. If the current account is in surplus（盈余）, the country's net international asset position increases correspondingly. Equally, a deficit（逆差）decreases the net international asset position.

The trade balance is identical to the difference between a country's output and its domestic demand (the difference between what goods a country produces and how many goods it buys from abroad; this does not include money re-spend on foreign stock, nor does it factor in the concept of importing goods to produce for the domestic market).

Measuring the balance of trade can be problematic because of the problems with recording and collecting data. As an illustration of this problem, when official data for all the world's countries are added up, exports exceed imports by almost 1%; it appears the world is running a positive balance of trade with itself. This cannot be true, because all transactions involve an equal credit or debit（借方）in the account of each nation. The discrepancy（差异）is widely believed to be explained by transactions intended to launder money（洗钱）or evade taxes（偷税漏税）, smuggling（走私）and other visibility problems. Especially for developing countries, the transaction statistics are likely to be inaccurate.

Factors that can affect the balance of trade include: the cost of production (land, labour, capital, taxes, incentives, etc.) in the exporting economy vis-à-vis those in the importing economy; the cost and availability of raw materials, intermediate goods（中间商品）and other inputs; currency exchange rate movements; multilateral, bilateral and unilateral taxes or restrictions on trade; non-tariff barriers such as environmental, health or safety standards; the availability of adequate foreign exchange with which to pay for imports; and prices of goods manufactured at home (influenced by the responsiveness of supply).

Text B Quotation

A customer has received a quotation from Krallpack. The following is the attachment and Todd's note.

	In der Loh 47
	407149 Düsseldorf
Date: 18.04.12	Tel +49 (0)211 - 10 07 98 67
To: Al Shamai Dairy	Fax + 49 (0)211 - 10 07 98 65
FAO: Jaleel Al Fahim	email: sales@krallpack.com

Dear Mr. Al Fahim
Re: Parts Quotation for SM300/Machine type 3000.002.93
Thank you for your enquiry. We are pleased to quote as the quotation form goes.

Qty	Description	Parts No	Unit Price
100	Tension spring	RZ-0531 9907.15	
10	Starting disc	3000.010.19	
4	Grooved bearing	6007-2RS1 9908	
1	Level switch	WF02	

Could you write back to Krallpack and order their spares? Could you also ask how much the extra costs will be and how long they'll take to get here? Thanks, Todd

The above prices are quoted in euros and are ex works in Korea. These prices do not include packing, transport, insurance and VAT. Our standard terms and conditions apply. The parts would be ready for despatch from Busan approximately four weeks after receipt of the order.
Kind regards

Gisela Mason

Gisela Mason
Krallpack

Unit 6 Trading

Words and expressions

apply	/əˈplaɪ/	v.	适用	part	/pɑːt/	n.	零件
approximately	/əˈprɒksɪmətlɪ/	adv.	大约	receipt	/rɪˈsiːt/	n.	接收
description	/dɪˈskrɪpʃn/	n.	说明	ex works			工厂交货；工厂交货价
despatch	/dɪˈspætʃ/	v.	发送	machine type			机型

Comprehension tasks

Read the text and choose the best phrase to complete each sentence.

1. The customer would like to
   a. buy some spare parts for a machine.
   b. buy a new packing machine.
   c. enquire about a new machine.
2. The letter is in reply to a
   a. confirmation of an order.
   b. request for information.
   c. letter of complaint.
3. The customer has to pay
   a. no extra costs.   b. only import tax.   c. all extra costs.
4. The order could
   a. leave the factory in about four weeks.
   b. be delivered in about four weeks.
   c. leave the factory immediately.

Paraphrase the following sentences.

1. The above prices are quoted in euros and are ex works in Korea.
2. Our standard terms and conditions apply.

Vocabulary

TASK 3 Complete each sentence with the appropriate preposition.

1. The company was registered __on__ 16 May 2003.
2. We last met _____ the Milan Trade Fair.
3. I hope to see you _____ Easter.
4. Business is usually quite quiet _____ the winter.
5. Imports rose by 3% _____ January.
6. The consignment is due to arrive in Hamburg _____ Saturday.
7. The shipment is due to arrive in Rotterdam _____ 18 September.
8. I don't think we'll have time _____ Friday afternoon.
9. We met him _____ Mr. West's retirement party.
10. We broke several export records _____ 2011.
11. The courier should be here to pick the goods up _____ a couple of hours.
12. We even kept the office open _____ Christmas Day this year.

TASK 4 Complete the word diagram with the following items related to transport in the box.

~~cargo~~	ferry	harbour	motorway	airport	frontier	dock
lorry	highway	truck	air freight	railway	container ship
port	station	border	shipping	air terminal

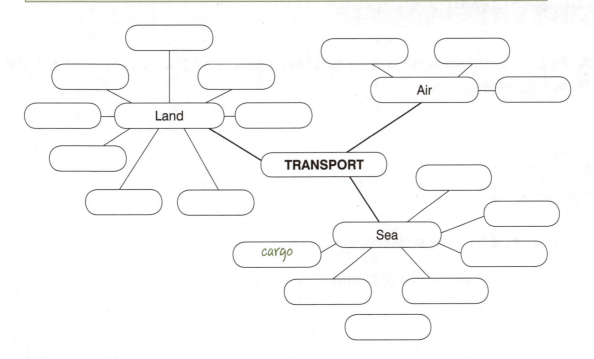

Which word is the odd one out?

1. consignment   packet   parcel   instalment
2. duty   fee   margin   fare
3. distribution   despatch   distance   delivery
4. discount   sale   offer   refund
5. schedule   timetable   itinerary postage
6. deadline   fine   penalty   charge
7. invoice   permit   licence   visa
8. petrol   fuel   gasoline   litre

Speaking

Work in pairs. Ask your partner questions and write a fact file for a company he/she knows.

Form a pair and discuss the following topic with your partner.

How to become a successful import agent

Business communication

Work in pairs. Search the Internet about some successful trading companies and discuss their businesses.

Translation

Translate the following sentences into Chinese.

1. The above prices are quoted in euros and are ex works in Korea.

2. The parts would be ready for despatch from Busan approximately four weeks after receipt of the order.

3. Rising import costs contributed to a slight increase in the company's prices across the board in May.

4. Nations usually produce and export those goods in which they have the greatest comparative advantage, and import those items in which they have the least comparative advantage.

5. Assuming the laboratory tests go well, and you can quote us a competitive price, we would certainly be able to make substantial orders on a regular basis.

Translate the following sentences into English.

1. 我希望此报价能为贵公司所接收，并有机会与贵公司展开合作。（quotation）

2. 如果您同意我们的建议，请草拟条款，我们将根据条款准备即将与专门代理商签订的协议。（term）

3. 感谢您的付款。您的物品将于周一从北京发货。（despatch）

4. 消费性经济大约占据了美国经济活动的 2/3。（approximately）

5. 货物数量与质量的验收应在买方收到货物后的14天内进行。（receipt）

Writing

Work in pairs. Read **Text B** again and write a reply to KrallPack. Plan your letter carefully with your partner before you write it.

UNIT 7 Delivery services

Warming up

TASK 1 The past decade has witnessed the booming growth of express industry. Why can this industry achieve such development in your view?

TASK 2 Work in pairs and discuss the current development of Chinese delivery industry.

Text A Parcel carriers

The following are the pages in the ParcelExpress CH brochure.

ParcelExpress CH—Parcels to the people

We are one of the world's fastest-growing and most dynamic package distribution companies with an annual revenue of €3 billion. As leading operators in the express parcels sector, we offer a range of specialist solutions and services and have an outstanding record in customer service. We employ 59,200 people in 150 countries and operate more than 35,000 vehicles from over 80 locations. Our customers understand our commitment to quality service and trust us to deliver over four million of their parcels across the world every day.

ParcelExpress CH is recognised as one of the most innovative parcel carrier companies in operation today. We have won many awards for our services particularly in the e-commerce sector. We are particularly well-known for our "Expect" service, which gives home shoppers a two-hour window of time in which their parcel will arrive. So customers don't have to stay at home all day waiting for the courier to come. The ParcelExpress CH call centres are listed in the top ten best call centres in Europe and offer the highest quality customer service in the industry.

Services

Express Priority Plus
This is ParcelExpress CH's fastest services for your most urgent documents and packages. It guarantees delivery by 8:30 a.m. the next day to hundreds of cities across Europe and Central Asia. The service also includes automatic confirmation of delivery by email as soon as your shipment is delivered.

Express Priority
This is the ideal service for your urgent deliveries. It guarantees delivery by 10:30 a.m. the next business day to over 200 countries. Full electronic tracking means confirmation of delivery is available within minutes in many cases.

Express Expedited
Express Expedited offers quality, reliability and scheduled delivery for your less urgent shipments. The service guarantees door-to-door deliveries within forty-eight hours. Full electronic tracking means confirmation of delivery is available within minutes in many cases.

Express Standard
The ParcelExpress CH Standard offers the benefits of ParcelExpress CH quality.

Words and expressions

commitment	/kəˈmɪtmənt/	n. 承诺；许诺	scheduled /ˈskedʒuːld/	adj. 预定的；预先安排的
dynamic	/daɪˈnæmɪk/	adj. 动态的；不断变化的	shipment /ˈʃɪpmənt/	n. 装运；运输的货物
e-commerce	/ˈiːkɒmɜːs/	n. 电子商务	automatic confirmation	自动确认
expedite	/ˈekspɪdaɪt/	v. 迅速完成；加速	customer service	客户服务
guarantee	/ˌɡærənˈtiː/	v. 保证；担保	door-to-door delivery	逐户分送
innovative	/ˈɪnəveɪtɪv/	adj. 创新的，有创新精神的	electronic tracking	电子跟踪
priority	/praɪˈɒrəti/	n. 优先；优先权		

Comprehension tasks

 Read the first part of the Parcel Express CH brochure. Complete the information about ParcelExpress CH with the figures below.

2   59,200   3 billion   35,000   10   4 million

1. Its turnover is more than _____ euro a year.
2. ParcelExpress CH delivers _____ parcels and documents every day.
3. The company owns _____ vehicles (cars, vans, trailers, etc.).
4. The ParcelExpress CH customer service centres are listed in the top _____ best call centres in Europe.
5. Home shoppers know the exact time within _____ hours when their ParcelExpress CH parcel will arrive.
6. The company employs about _____ people worldwide.

 Read the text again and match the phrases with one of the features of the services.

1. Only our Express Priority Plus guarantees…
2. Three services provide…
3. With the Express Expedited service, you can arrange…
4. Both Express Priority Plus and Express Priority guarantee…

> a. same day delivery
> b. next day delivery
> c. delivery to only E.U. countries
> d. next day delivery by 8:30 a.m.
> e. confirmation of delivery
> f. worldwide next day delivery by 10:30 a.m.
> g. delivery on a particular day

Vocabulary

 Read through the brochure again and find examples of the following:

- words and phrases that are repeated several times;
- words and phrases written to impress the reader.

TASK 4 Match the following sentence halves by use of linking lines.

1. Don't worry, an Express Expedited parcel will arrive in — 3:30.
2. An Express Priority parcel will get there within — two days.
3. To arrive tomorrow, the package needs to leave by — on time.
4. I'll stay here until — in time.
5. It arrived at 8:30, which was exactly — twenty-four hours.
6. We sent it by ParcelExpress CH Premium so it should arrive — ParcelExpress CH collects the parcel.

TASK 5 Complete the following sentences with the prepositions in the box.

| in | on | by | until | within |

1. We sent it by Express Priority Plus so it should arrive _____ 8:30 tomorrow morning.
2. We chose ParcelExpress CH Expedited in order to guarantee delivery _____ twenty-four hours.
3. She's very punctual. She always arrives exactly _____ time.
4. If you email it, it'll get there _____ minutes.
5. We can't send it _____ we've weighed it.
6. If you want delivery _____ a particular day, you should request a scheduled delivery.
7. It needs to arrive _____ tomorrow so we'll have to send it Express Priority.
8. Please wait _____ I inform you that I have received the package.

Listening and speaking

TASK 6 Listen and complete the following sentences.

1. Chinese delivery industry experienced a sound development at the rate of _____ every year.
2. At present, there are more than _____ express enterprises in China.
3. There are a lot of problems with small family businesses because they only _____ on their own interests instead of the long-term development of the whole industry.

Work in pairs and discuss the following questions.

How many express companies have you ever cooperated with? What are they? Which one do you think provide the best services?

Business communication

 Work in pairs. Which three of the following features do you think are the most important for a parcel delivery service?

| next day delivery | reliability | confirmation of delivery |
| global network | low prices | high quality of service |

Translation

 Translate the following sentences into Chinese.

1. We are one of the world's fastest-growing and most dynamic package distribution companies with an annual revenue of €3 billion.

2. As leading operators in the express parcels sector, we offer a range of specialist solutions and services and have an outstanding record in customer service.

3. Full electronic tracking means confirmation of delivery is available within minutes in many cases.

4. The delivery of goods will be automatically confirmed by an email once your shipment is delivered.

5. SF Express has been listed in the top three logistics companies in China because of its quality express services for customers.

Translate the following sentences into English.

1. 广告收入在新财年取得了开门红。(revenue)

2. 公司久负盛名的品牌并不能确保商品的质量。(guarantee)

3. 他感觉这些缩减措施和政府提高教育水平的承诺背道而驰。(commitment)

4. 这个商店提供一些廉价的商品，但是其数量不能满足周围不富足居民的需求。(available)

5. 定期航班的数量让空中交通指挥系统不堪重负。(scheduled)

Writing

 Suppose you just received a package which was delivered days after the scheduled time and was heavily damaged. Write a complaint letter to the express company:

- making detailed descriptions of the condition of your package;
- claiming for a compensation;
- giving your advice for their delivery service.

Business know-how

Read the following passage and make an oral summary of the main points to your partner or group.

Contract（合同）

A contract is a promise or set of promises that are legally enforceable and, if violated（违反）, allow the injured party access to legal remedies（补偿）. Contract law recognises and governs the rights and duties arising from agreements. In the Anglo-American common law, formation of a contract generally requires an offer, acceptance, consideration, and a mutual intent to be bound. Each party must have capacity to enter the contract.

In order for a contract to be formed, the parties must reach mutual assent (also called a meeting of the minds). This is typically reached through offer and an acceptance which does not vary the offer's terms, which is known as the "mirror image rule". An offer is a definite statement of the offeror's willingness to be bound in certain conditions. If a purported (声称的) acceptance does vary the terms of an offer, it is not an acceptance but a counteroffer (还价) and, therefore, simultaneously a rejection of the original offer.

A concept of English common law, consideration is required for simple contracts but not for special contracts (contracts by deed). The court in *Currie v Misa* declared consideration to be a "Right, Interest, Profit, Benefit, or Forbearance (暂缓行驶), Detriment (损害), Loss, Responsibility". Thus, consideration is a promise of something of value given by a promissor in exchange for something of value given by a promisee; and typically the thing of value is goods, money, or an act. Forbearance to act, such as an adult promising to refrain from smoking, is enforceable only if one is thereby surrendering a legal right.

A mutual intent to be bound (also referred to as mutual assent) is a phrase in contract law used to describe the intentions of the parties forming the contract. In particular, it refers to the situation where there is a common understanding in the formation of the contract. Formation of a contract is initiated with a proposal or offer. This condition or element is considered a requirement to the formation of a contract in some jurisdictions (审判权；管辖权).

Text B Sending a parcel

The following is the guide of sending a parcel in the ParcelExpress CH brochure.

How to use the guide

All shipping charges are based on three criteria: the service selected, the weight of the shipment and the zone number for the destination. To find the correct rate for your shipment, follow these three steps:

1 Choose your service
ParcelExpress CH offers a choice of Express Priority Expedited or Standard. Refer to the zone chart to see which services are available.

2 Choose the zone
Find the destination country and find its zone number.

3 Find the rate
Turn to the rate chart and match the shipment rate with the correct zone number.

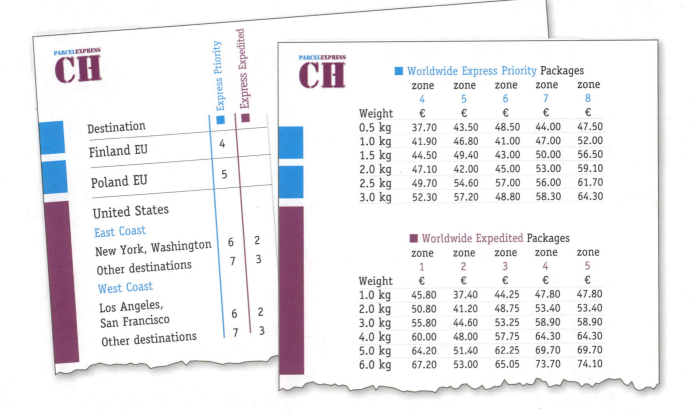

Words and expressions

criteria /kraɪˈtɪərɪə/   *n.* 标准；准则（criterion 的复数）

destination /ˌdestɪˈneɪʃən/   *n.* 目的地

selected /sɪˈlektɪd/   *adj.* 经由选择的；挑选的

shipping /ˈʃɪpɪŋ/   *n.* 运送

Comprehension tasks

 Suppose a company in the U.K. wants to send three packages to different countries. How much will each item cost according to the text?

Weight: 3000g
To: Helsinki
To arrive by tomorrow morning

Weight: 1200g
To: Warsaw
To arrive within 48 hours

Weight: 2400g
To: United States Seattle
To arrive Thursday

Unit 7 Delivery services   113

Work in pairs. Read the text again. Suppose you want to send a package to your friend abroad. Please write down the weight, destination and the arrival time you expect of your package and invite your partner to answer how much it will cost.

Vocabulary

 Complete the following sentences with the words in the box.

| destinations | urgent | charge | weight |
| documents | packages | vehicles | rate |

1. ParcelExpress CH will deliver both your _____ and parcels.
2. If you have the zone and the weight, you can work out the delivery _____.
3. Most ParcelExpress CH delivery _____ are vans.
4. You can send really _____ parcels to arrive before 8:30 a.m. the following day.
5. There is a standard postal _____ for E.U. countries.
6. They deliver to _____ in almost every country.
7. It is more expensive to send heavy _____ by post than by parcel delivery services.
8. The cost of the service depends on the _____ of the package and the speed of the service.

TASK 4 Read the following information and choose the correct option to complete each sentence.

1. For additional charges, please refer to Page 10.

   You should turn to Page Ten
   a. to see about possible discounts.
   b. to find out about extra costs.
   c. for information about the product.

2. Guaranteed delivery within forty-eight hours.

   The parcel will arrive
   a. in less than two days from now.
   b. in exactly two days' time.
   c. in at least two days' time.

3. **Export documentation may be required for non-E.U. destinations.**

   Packages sent outside the E.U.
   a. must be documents only.
   b. will need special documents.
   c. might need special documents.

4. **Payment to be made by cash on delivery.**

   The invoice has to be paid
   a. after the shipment arrives.
   b. before the shipment arrives.
   c. when the shipment arrives.

5. **Transport papers must include an approximate value of the shipment.**

   The transport documents have to show
   a. how much the shipment is worth.
   b. the delivery charges for the shipment.
   c. a list of what is in the shipment.

TASK 5

Complete each sentence with the appropriate preposition.

1. The parcel was delivered _____ a young courier.
2. It was a real race _____ time to get this job done.
3. _____ one third of the packages were damaged due to the heavy rain.
4. The express company will have delivered 200 million packages _____ the end of this year.
5. The party was held _____ the setting up of a new package centre.
6. The express industry develops fast _____ the rise of online shopping.
7. An email of automatic confirmation will be sent _____ you when the deal is done.
8. The courier called him to pick _____ his parcel.
9. They will arrive _____ London on Monday for a business meeting.
10. When we arrived _____ the express centre, they had been off duty.

Speaking

TASK 6

Work in pairs. Talk to your partner about the advantages and disadvantages of today's parcel delivery service.

Form a pair and discuss the following topic with your partner.

Suppose you and your partner are in different companies. Talk to your partner about what kind of parcel delivery service your company uses and why? Or you may talk about how much your company spends in sending documents and parcels, and where the destinations are.

Business communication

 Work in pairs. What other ways are there to send documents and parcels abroad? What are the advantages and disadvantages of each method?

Translation

 Translate the following sentences into Chinese.

1. To find the correct rate for your shipment, follow these three steps.

2. Turn to the rate chart and match the shipment rate with the correct zone number.

3. All shipping charges are based on three criteria: the service selected, the weight of the shipment and the zone number for the destination.

4. Express company usually provides different types of express services because of the different modes and objects of transportation.

5. China's express industry is currently in an environment of fierce competition between domestic express companies and international express giants.

 Translate the following sentences into English.

1. 几部让人翘首企盼的录像片将在这个月到货。(arrive)

2. 这位消费者被诈取了服务费。(charge)

3. 银行正在重新评估其贷款标准。(criteria)

4. 仅有一半的紧急救援物资运抵目的地。(destination)

5. 抵制通货膨胀比抑制日益加剧的经济衰退更为重要。(priority)

Writing

Task 11 Suppose your company is going to ship a large number of goods to an overseas buyer. Write an email to Mr. Joans, a manager in a delivery company, to ask about details of shipping goods and relevant charges. You may tell him the category, weight, volume and other necessary information about your goods.

UNIT 8 Recruiting staff

Warming up

 Work in pairs. How many different ways can a company recruit applicants to fill a job vacancy?

 Choose the best word to complete each sentence.

1. We had over thirty **applicants/assistants** for the vacancy we advertised in the local paper.
2. I had to fill in a **CV/an application form** and return it to the HR Department.
3. We **appointed/filled** someone to the position over two weeks ago.
4. We advertised the **employment/vacancy** on the Internet.
5. We need to **apply/recruit** ten more people before summer.
6. I am going to the interview the **candidates/appointments** tomorrow.

Text A Advertising a vacancy

The following are two advertisements about the vacancy at Goldsmiths.

To: All offices
From: Rick Hayward
Date: 6 March 2012
Re: Vacancy for Senior Marketing Assistant

Senior Marketing Assistant—London

Goldsmiths Holidays has a vacancy at its main London offices for an assistant to the Marketing Director.

The successful candidate will be a graduate with at least three years' marketing experience and preferably a second European language. Key responsibilities will include helping to plan and manage our range of package holidays and building relationships with partners.

If you wish to apply for the vacancy, please speak with your office manager and contact Rick Hayward at Heath Villas by 13 March.

requires a
Senior Marketing Assistant

Goldsmiths, one of Europe's largest package holiday companies, requires a **Senior Marketing Assistant** at our main London offices. Working closely with the Marketing Director, you will help plan and manage our range of quality products and maintain relationships with our partners worldwide.

A confident and skilled communicator, you will be a graduate with a minimum of three years' marketing experience within the travel industry. A second European language would also be an advantage.

The rewards in terms of salary, benefits and career development will fully reflect your contribution to the success of Goldsmiths Holidays Ltd.

If you think you have the ability and the confidence, please email your CV to: Goldsmiths Holidays, 24 Heath Villas, The Vale of Heath, London NW3 1AW.
email: refsma@goldsmiths.com

Words and expressions

advertisement	/ˌædvəˈtaɪzmənt/	*n.*	广告	preferably	/ˈprefərəblɪ/	*adv.*	更好地
confident	/ˈkɒnfɪdənt/	*adj.*	自信的	reward	/rɪˈwɔːd/	*n.*	奖励，奖赏
contribution	/ˌkɒntrɪˈbjuːʃən/	*n.*	贡献	senior	/ˈsiːnjə(r)/	*adj.*	高级的
graduate	/ˈɡrædʒuət/	*n.*	大学毕业生	apply for			申请；请求
minimum	/ˈmɪnɪməm/	*n.*	最小值；最低限度	in terms of			在……方面

Comprehension tasks

 Read the two advertisements and answer the following questions.

1. Where would the advertisements appear?
2. How is the information organised in the two advertisements?
3. What extra information does the newspaper advertisement include?
4. Which advertisement tries to "sell" the position more? How?
5. What are the main responsibilities of this senior Marketing Assistant?

 Read the text again and circle "True" or "False". Correct the false sentences.

1. Goldsmiths Holidays has a vacancy for Senior Marketing Assistant with at least five years, marketing experience. True/False
2. The successful candidate should be a graduate essentially with a second European language. True/False
3. Senior Marketing Assistant should work closely with the Marketing Director and will have the final right to plan and manage the company's range of package holidays. True/False
4. The Senior Marketing Assistant is expected to be a confident and skilled communicator with marketing experience within the travel industry. True/False
5. Details of the rewards in terms of salary, benefits and career development are clearly reflected in the recruitment notice. True/False

Vocabulary

TASK 3 Match the personal characteristics with their definitions by use of linking lines.

1. bossy
2. capable
3. careful
4. careless
5. cheerful
6. confident
7. experienced
8. helpful
9. lazy
10. punctual

a. always makes time to assist colleagues
b. likes to tell others what to do
c. has done the job for many years
d. does not work very hard
e. does everything very well
f. is always happy at work
g. makes a lot of mistakes
h. always arrives on time
i. does not worry about things being difficult
j. tries very hard not to make mistakes

Complete the table. Then use the correct form of the words to complete the sentences below.

adjective	noun
skilled	skill
_____	absenteeism
ill	_____
punctual	_____
_____	anxiety
angry	_____
_____	qualifications
retired	_____

1. There seems to be a real shortage of ___skilled___ workers on the job market at the moment.
2. She was quite _____ during the interview. She looked very nervous.
3. You'll need to bring proof of your _____ to the interview—for example any certificates or diplomas.
4. We have a real _____ problem. We're losing about 200 working days a month with people being off work for one reason or another.
5. There's an infection going around the office so a lot of staff are off _____.
6. Many people take early _____ in their 50s, creating a lot of vacancies.
7. We don't really have to worry about being _____ as the company operates a flexitime system.
8. I was really quite _____ when they told me in the interview that the job had already been given to someone else.

Unit 8 Recruiting staff 123

TASK 5 Match the verbs with the nouns by use of linking lines. Then use them in the correct form to complete the sentences below.

apply for — your resignation
turn down — a job
take on   salary levels
select   vacancies
fill in   staff
review   a candidate
hand in   an offer
advertise   an application form

1. There's no way we can interview all the candidates who __apply for a job__.
2. Congratulations on the job offer. The boss is going to get a shock when you _____. I'd love to see his face when you do it!
3. We normally _____ from a shortlist of about four or five people.
4. The company's been doing very well recently and is now looking to expand and _____ sometime early next year.
5. We're finding it very hard to keep our IT people at the moment, so I think we're going to have to _____ to try and keep them with the company.
6. I got a letter from the Personnel Manager asking me to _____ and return it with my CV and a photograph.
7. If it's for the Web Department, it's only really natural to _____ on the website. That's where the people we need will be looking.
8. These days graduates can't afford to _____. The job market is so competitive that any job is worth considering.

Listening

TASK 6 Two HR managers discuss the vacancy at Goldsmiths. Listen to the conversation. Which advertisement do they decide to place first? Why?

TASK 7 Listen to the conversation again. What are the disadvantages of each type of advertisement?

Business communication

Work in pairs. How would your partner recruit people if he/she were a HR manager (internal recruitment or social recruitment)?

Translation

Translate the following sentences into Chinese.

1. The successful candidate will be a graduate with at least three years' marketing experience and preferably a second European language.

2. Key responsibilities will include helping to plan and manage our range of package holidays and building relationships with partners.

3. Before being able to apply for a better position, he is to be a junior member in the company.

4. Mr. Smith of your company has told me that your department needs a manager assistant, and I wish to apply for the position.

5. Even though unemployment rate has been decreasing since 2000, wages didn't increase, and low wages have been a leading factor for dissatisfaction in the workplace.

Translate the following sentences into English.

1. 每年的大学毕业生人数都在不断增加。(graduate)

2. 公司人事部门的一大职责就是给公司招聘到合适的人才。(responsibility)

3. 申请这份工作的人寥寥无几。(apply for)

4. 他工作一直很努力，为公司做出了许多贡献。(contribution)

5. 公司规定所有员工须按时上班。(require)

Writing

Write a job advertisement for English teachers. It should include information such as job description, responsibilities, requirements for English proficiency and educational background.

Business know-how

Read the following passage and make an oral summary of the main points to your partner or group.

Recruitment (招聘)

Recruitment (hiring) refers to the overall process of attracting, selecting and appointing suitable candidates for jobs (either permanent or temporary) within an organisation. Recruitment can also refer to processes involved in choosing individuals for unpaid roles. Managers, human resource generalists (多面手) and recruitment specialists may be tasked with carrying out recruitment, but in some cases public-sector employment agencies, commercial recruitment agencies, or specialist search consultancies are used to undertake parts of the process. Internet-based technologies to support all aspects of recruitment have become widespread.

Internal recruitment refers to the process of a candidate being selected from the existing workforce to take up a new job in the same organisation, perhaps as a promotion, or to provide career development opportunity, or to meet a specific or urgent organisational need. Advantages include the organisation's familiarity with the employees and their competencies insofar as they are revealed in their current job. It can be quicker and have a lower cost to hire someone internally.

Social recruitment (social hiring or social media recruitment) is recruiting candidates by using social platforms as talent databases (数据库) or for advertising. Social recruiting uses social media profiles (简介), blogs, and other Internet sites to find information on candidates. It also uses social media to advertise jobs either through HR vendors or through crowdsourcing (众包) where job seekers and others share job openings within their online social networks.

Text B Recruitment methods

The following is a magazine article about recruiting staff.

PROFILE

The right person for the right job

Finding the right job applicant to fill a vacancy is never easy. **Julie Bain** *looks at the pros and cons of different recruitment methods.*

Recruiting the right candidate to fill a vacancy can be a difficult and costly task. Appointing the wrong person could be an expensive mistake which could cause personnel problems for the whole department. And, as every HR Manager knows, it is much more difficult to get rid of someone than it is to employ them.

The HR Manager's first decision is whether to recruit internal applicants or advertise the vacancy outside the company. Internal applicants are easy to recruit by memo, email or newsletter. Furthermore, they are easy to assess and know the company well. However, they rarely bring fresh ideas to a position. Moreover, a rejected internal candidate might become unhappy and leave the company.

Recruiting outside the company means either advertising the vacancy directly or using an employment agency. If the company decides to advertise the vacancy directly, it has to decide where to place the advertisement. Traditionally this has meant newspapers and professional journals but now the Internet is also very popular. The decision normally depends on the vacancy. Companies advertise blue-collar or clerical jobs in local newspapers and senior management positions in national papers or professional journals, while the Internet is one of the best ways of advertising IT vacancies or recruiting abroad. However, with the Internet there is a risk of receiving unsuitable applications from all over the world.

An employment agency can be either a private business or a local government employment centre. A company often uses a local government employment agency to recruit blue-collar workers but normally prefers a commercial agency for its white-collar staff. However, a commercial agency could be very expensive and the applicants are less likely to stay with the company for a long time.

Words and expressions

appoint /əˈpɔɪnt/	v. 任命；委派	newsletter /ˈnjuːzletə(r)/ n.	通讯；简报
blue-collar /ˌbluː ˈkɒlə(r)/	adj. 蓝领阶级的，从事体力劳动的	personnel /ˌpɜːsəˈnel/ adj.	人员的；有关人事的
clerical /ˈklerɪkl/	adj. 办公室工作的	rarely /ˈreəli/ adv.	很少；罕有
internal /ɪnˈtɜːnl/	adj. 内部的	unsuitable /ʌnˈsuːtəbl/ adj.	不适合的；不适宜的
memo /ˈmeməʊ/	n. 便条；备忘录	get rid of	摆脱；除去
		pros and cons	利弊；正反两方面

Comprehension tasks

 Read the text and complete the following diagram.

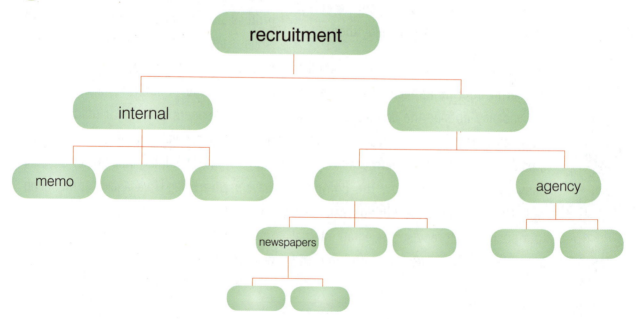

Look at the following extracts from the article and answer the questions.

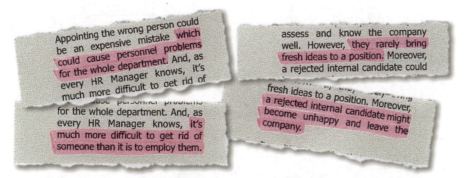

1. How could the wrong candidate cause problems for the whole department?
2. Why is it difficult to get rid of someone?
3. Why don't internal applicants have fresh ideas?
4. Why might an unsuccessful candidate leave the company?
5. If you were the HR manager, what would you do to motivate internal candidates to bring more fresh ideas and make them happy to stay?

Vocabulary

 Complete the following sentences with the words and phrase in the box.

| get rid of | recruitment | memo | commercial | appoint |

1. The HR manager spends a lot of time thinking about talent _____.
2. He needed to move on with his life and _____ the huge financial burden.
3. The company is seeking to _____ a new director-general.
4. I sent him a(an) _____ to remind him about the meeting.
5. His mission was to secure a series of important _____ agreements.

 Complete the word diagram with the following items related to job interviews.

personal details	benefits	hobbies	qualifications	holiday allowance
covering letter	salary	skills	career prospects	
application form	referees	experience	certificates	

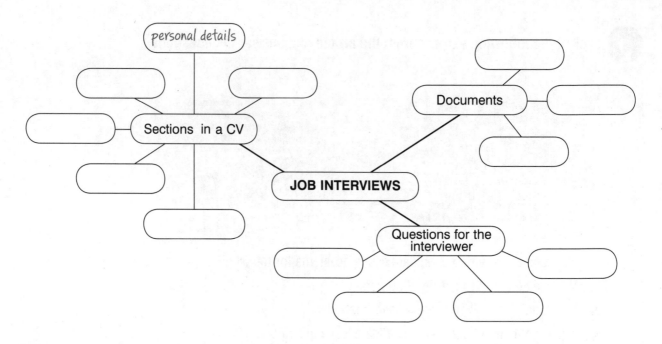

TASK 5 Match the words with a similar meaning by use of linking lines.

1. unemployed   a. select
2. temporary   b. evaluate
3. fire   c. short-term
4. appoint   d. pay
5. act   e. dismiss
6. reward   f. capable
7. assess   g. behave
8. skilled   h. out of work

Speaking

TASK 6 Work in pairs. How would you advertise the following vacancies?

| finance director | graphic designer | marketing manager |
| truck driver | bilingual secretary | computer programmer |

TASK 7 Form a pair and discuss the following topic with your partner.

The advantages and disadvantages of internal recruitment

Business communication

Find a partner and ask where he/she plans to find a job vacancy and how to apply for it. And share your own ideas with your partner.

Translation

Translate the following sentences into Chinese.

1. Recruiting the right candidate to fill a vacancy can be a difficult and costly task.

2. Appointing the wrong person could be an expensive mistake which could cause personnel problems for the whole department.

3. Recruiting outside the company means either advertising the vacancy directly or using an employment agency.

4. A good recruitment strategy is a pivotal (关键的) aspect of procuring and retaining high-quality talents.

5. Recruitment can be conducted internally through the promotion of current employees.

Translate the following sentences into English.

1. 新成立的公司往往有很多空缺的职位。(vacancy)

2. 他工作很努力，能力也很强，很快就被任命为部门领导。(appoint)

3. 公司的订单量增加了，需要雇佣更多工人。(employ)

4. 每份工作都有其优缺点。(pros and cons)

5. 招聘一位新的经理可能会让公司摆脱这场危机。(get rid of)

Writing

 Suppose you are going to find a job. Write your own resume in English.

Part I Listening comprehension

TASK 1 Coca-Cola CEO and incoming chairman James Quincey sits down with CNBC's Sara Eisen. Listen to their talk about the Coca-Cola brand and the economic uncertainty. Fill in each blank. You will hear the talk TWICE.

1. Mr. Quincey said in the market, there is a normal level of _____ , which is a sign of uncertainty.
2. It seems that Mr. Quincey still holds a positive view into _____ .
3. According to Mr. Quincey, Coca-Cola took _____ at the beginning of summer given the process of some inflation in the U.S. market.
4. _____ of uncertainty is gonna be in growth next year in the U.S. and in global economy.
5. On behalf of Coca-Cola, Mr. Quincey said they are _____ on the plan to develop the market.

TASK 2 Listen to a news report and decide whether the statements are "True" or "False". You will hear the news report TWICE.

1. That the number of shoppers visiting retailers on Boxing Day has fallen for the third year could be attributed to sluggish economy and the rise of Internet shopping.   True/False
2. Sales in shopping centres, high streets and retail parks were up only in London.   True/False
3. Boxing Day has become less important as a trading day.   True/False
4. According to Diane Wehrle, the growth of online sales is as much this year as last year.   True/False
5. Consumers nowadays are so used to being lured with promotions that price cuts of 20% or 30% are of little avail.   True/False

TASK 3 Listen to a clip of the interpretation of President Xi's speech in Davos, 2017 and answer the following questions. You will hear the clip TWICE.

1. What did the speaker mean by quoting "It was the best of times and it was the worst of times." at the beginning?
2. What is the point made by President Xi about the criticism of economic globalisation?
3. According to the speech, what is the most pressing task for us now?

Part II Reading and writing

Read the following passage and choose the correct answer to each question.

The e-commerce revolution has turned the "traditional" supply chain on its head. From speed to delivery, to increased expectations for the delivery experience, this change has in large part been driven by the more empowered consumer of today. However, it is in the last-mile that many of these challenges manifest. Here are four challenges that are most prominent:

Cost

Cost is not a new issue, but a new expectation, particularly regarding same-day/on-demand delivery has put a greater strain on budgets. Additionally, when it comes to online retail, there can be inconsistent demand, such as increasingly higher volumes of purchases during holidays.

There is no silver bullet for offsetting costs. However, efficiency and planning go a long way to neutralise its effect. For bigger e-commerce companies such as Amazon, creating efficiencies throughout the supply chain enable lower costs during the last-mile.

Transparency

In the modern on-demand era, tracking code doesn't satisfy consumers any more—they want to have full, real-time visibility over their deliveries. In particular, they want to see the entirety of the last-mile.

Though initially for taxis, Uber gives customers the ability to have full visibility over where their driver is. Customers can follow the driver through a real-time map to know exactly when they arrive. Now, consumers are starting to expect this kind of visibility for all services, including deliveries.

Efficiency

Customers have been the major driving force for increased efficiency. Among other reasons, the requirement for increased efficiency is predicated on the desire for faster deliveries. On-demand has penetrated every industry and business, and online retail is no exception.

Efficiency can be increased throughout the supply chain, but when talking about the last mile, especially with regards to same-day/on-demand delivery, technology is the key. Things such as automatically despatching to the right delivery person, in the right area, at the right time can help increase efficiency and decrease delivery time.

Friction

A frictionless delivery experience helps streamline efficiency and cut costs. One of the greatest sources of friction during last mile delivery is dealing with customer inquiries about their delivery and requests about how it should be delivered.

Creating a frictionless delivery process requires technology that enables open communication between the customer and the delivery person, as well as full visibility over their deliveries. By doing so, you lessen the likelihood of a customer calling in and having to deal with a customer service representative.

1. Which of the following is the best title for the passage?
   a. The importance for e-commerce development.
   b. Last mile delivery challenges for e-commerce.
   c. Supply chain challenges for e-commerce.
2. What does the underlined phrase "silver bullet" probably mean in the third paragraph?
   a. A bullet made of silver.
   b. A complicated problem.
   c. A magical solution.
3. Why can Uber satisfy the customers with a real-time map?
   a. Because they know where the taxis are.
   b. Because they know where their deliveries are.
   c. Because they get the visibility.
4. Which of the following is NOT mentioned in solving the last mile problem?
   a. Technology.   b. Supply chain.   c. Staffing policy.
5. What request do customers probably have about how goods should be delivered?
   a. Don't ring the door bell.
   b. Goods ordered have been delayed.
   c. Goods will be delivered tomorrow.

TASK 5 Read the list below. It shows the contents of a company's Annual Report. Decide in which part of the report (a–h) you would find the information (1–5). For each question, mark the correct letter a–h.

> **Stella Group Plc**
> **Annual Report**
> a. Chairman's Statement
> b. National Sales Reports
> c. Review of Subsidiaries
> d. Changes in Key Personnel
> e. Group Organigram
> f. Auditor's Report
> g. Profit and Loss Account
> h. Balance Sheet

1. A statement of the company's income and expenses.
2. The names of new executives and board members.
3. A look at the performance of smaller companies that Stella owns.
4. A list of what the company owns and owes.
5. A statement by the company that checked the financial reports.

Task 6 Read the newspaper article below about a new alliance in the packaging industry and choose the correct option.

The big number

The country's demand for mobile phones and on-line communication is growing at an increasingly fast rate. In fact, it is growing (1) ____ quickly that our telephone numbering system needs re-organising (2) ____ some major changes will have to (3) ____ made.

These changes, (4) ____ , will make the system simpler and easier to use. It is (5) ____ an important task that all the U.K. telecoms companies are working together to make (6) ____ changes. The changes will (7) ____ only make hundreds of millions of new numbers, but they will (8) ____ bring order and flexibility to the system for years to come.

(9) ____ main changes are due to happen (10) ____ now and the year 2014, which will give you (11) ____ of time to prepare. You will find details of the number changes on our website, (12) ____ you can visit any time at www.numberchange.org or call our freephone helpline on 0808 224 2000.

1. a. so	b. that	c. too	7. a. if	b. not	c. but
2. a. and	b. with	c. before	8. a. furthermore	b. additionally	c. also
3. a. been	b. be	c. being	9. a. The	b. Those	c. Their
4. a. despite	b. however	c. although	10. a. from	b. between	c. until
5. a. much	b. such	c. so	11. a. plenty	b. many	c. lot
6. a. this	b. there	c. these	12. a. when	b. who	c. which

 Task 7 Read the following email from a colleague and write a suitable letter to reply.

Gill

I'm on holiday next week so could I ask for a favour? I need to reply to a letter I got yesterday from a company called Network Schweiz—an IT service company looking for new business. Could you write back to them for me, ask for a price list and make an appointment for one of their people to come and see us some time when I'm back? The woman who wrote to me is Anja Ratzenberger. Her address is:

Network Schweiz
Neunbrunnenstr 18
8050 Zurich
Switzerland

Part III Business knowledge and translation

 Briefly define the following underlined business terms in English and translate each term into Chinese.

1. <u>VAT</u> and the Consumption Tax were levied and administered by the State competent departments of taxation, while the Business Tax was collected and administered by the local competent departments of taxation.
   Definition: _____
   Translation: _____

2. Banks are able to borrow at extremely cheap rates while charging borrowers more, giving them a tidy <u>profit margin</u>.
   Definition: _____
   Translation: _____

3. We have received your letter of July 23rd for insurance on the subject goods and the <u>premium</u> is to be borne by you.
   Definition: _____
   Translation: _____

4. It is important for you to read the "fine print" in any <u>insurance policy</u> so that you know what kind of coverage you are buying.
   Definition: _____
   Translation: _____

5. The <u>commission</u> will be out of the annual management fee and was viewed by some investors as dilutive to the other shareholders.
   Definition: _____
   Translation: _____

 Translate the following Chinese passage into English.

如今，电子通信技术的迅猛发展为公司建立良好的公共关系提供了各种传播工具。若要在激烈的市场竞争中立于不败之地，公司就必须制定与其发展目标配套的公关策略，建立一整套能灵活应对各种公关问题的长效机制。